THE STOIC WISDOM *of* MARCUS AURELIUS

Timeless Lessons on Control, Duty, and Inner Calm

RICHARD LAWSON

The Meditations were originally written in Greek. Where original passages appear in this book, a traditional Latin rendering is used. This is an editorial choice made for clarity and visual consistency.

Paperback ISBN: 978-1-961963-97-9
Published by Karma Studio
info@karmabookshelf.com

Contents

You have power over your mind,
not outside events.
Realize this, and you will find strength.

– Marcus Aurelius

Introduction

This book does not aim to make you calmer, wiser, or better than you already are. It's quieter than that.

It's written for readers already carrying responsibility, pressure, or uncertainty—people looking less for motivation than for steadiness. If you're reading this while managing more than you can easily resolve, these pages are meant to meet you there. Not to reassure or energize you, but to offer a steadier way of holding what's already on your plate.

No background in philosophy is required. No new identity or way of speaking is expected. Nothing here asks you to become someone else.

Marcus Aurelius wrote his reflections for himself, often when things were not going well. He wrote to remain aligned with his duties under demanding conditions and uncertain outcomes—not to explain a system, persuade an audience, or leave a legacy.

I've approached his writing in the same spirit. Each passage is treated as a practical reminder rather than a polished lesson. The aim is usefulness: the kind that helps you pause, clarify judgment, and return to what matters when attention is pulled in too many directions.

You'll find simple ideas, explained carefully and connected to ordinary situations most people recognize: work, responsibility, decision-making, frustration, restraint. Read slowly. Open anywhere. Return to the same ideas more than once. That's how Marcus used his own notes, and it remains the most natural way to read them.

The book begins by clarifying who Marcus Aurelius was and the conditions under which he wrote. With that context in place, everything that follows becomes easier to read—and easier to trust.

Sources and Translation

The passages attributed to Marcus Aurelius in this book are based on the *Meditations*, a text preserved through a long manuscript tradition and multiple Latin translations.

The English renderings presented here are interpretive, not literal. They aim at clarity, proportion, and practical use rather than strict word-for-word translation.

No single historical edition is treated as definitive. The text draws on established public-domain sources and later scholarly translations, compared and adjusted to reflect meaning rather than period style.

Any emphasis, phrasing, or structural choice reflects editorial judgment, not a claim to textual authority. The purpose is use under pressure, not academic precision.

PART I

HOW TO READ MARCUS AURELIUS TODAY

1

Who Marcus Aurelius Was (and Was Not)

Marcus Aurelius is often remembered as a philosopher.

But that was never his job.

He was an emperor of Rome, placed at the center of power and responsibility, expected to govern an enormous and unstable world. His days were shaped by decisions affecting millions—many made under pressure, with incomplete information, and rarely with the luxury of certainty.

He didn't retreat from life to think about it.

Life pressed in on him constantly.

War, politics, illness, betrayal, fatigue—these weren't distant concerns or abstract themes. They were his daily environment. Whatever philosophical reflection he practiced happened alongside duty, not instead of it, often in moments when duty felt heaviest.

This changes how we read his words.

Marcus didn't choose a quiet intellectual path and later comment on the world from a safe distance. He was immersed in the demands of leadership, carrying obligations he couldn't step away from, even when he wanted to. His thinking grew from necessity, not preference—from pressure rather than leisure.

He was writing for himself, not for an audience.

There's no evidence he intended to instruct others or shape a school of thought. He wasn't writing lessons, arguments, or carefully structured explanations for students. He was writing to himself—often in short bursts, often without polish, often when things were not going well.

What we now call *Meditations* was never meant to be a book. It was a collection of private notes, written over time, usually in moments of strain. Reminders. Corrections. Brief reflections meant to steady his own mind when it threatened to drift.

The tone makes this clear.

Repetitive. Sometimes blunt. Sometimes uneven. Ideas appear again and again, not because he wanted to persuade a reader, but because he needed to remind himself of things he already knew and still struggled to live by. The repetition reflects effort and friction, not literary style.

Marcus wasn't trying to sound wise.

He was trying to remain composed.

He wrote to hold himself to standards he feared he might fail to meet, especially when circumstances pushed him toward anger, fear, or impatience. Writing became a tool for self-command—something he returned to when the world around him felt unstable or overwhelming.

That's why the text feels different from works designed for an audience. No effort to impress. No concern for elegance. No attempt to build a complete system. Some thoughts are practical and grounded. Others feel almost impatient. Together, they show a person working through difficulty as it unfolds, not after it has passed.

Because the notes were private, they carry a particular kind of honesty. There was no benefit in pretending when no one else was meant to read them. The writing records not only confidence and resolve, but also doubt, irritation, repeated self-correction.

That honesty is part of why the text still feels relevant.

Marcus doesn't present himself as an ideal human being. He doesn't speak from a place of completion. He presents himself as someone who falls short, notices it, and tries again. The value lies in that effort, not in any claim of moral perfection.

This also explains why his reflections continue to speak to modern readers. The setting is ancient, but the pressures are familiar. Responsibility, expectation, fatigue, the weight of decision-making—none of this is tied to a particular era or social structure.

Many people today carry quieter versions of similar burdens.

They may lead teams, care for family members, or manage roles that leave little room for error. They may not rule an empire, but they live with consequences that matter—often without much recognition, with limited control over outcomes.

In situations like these, there's often a need for inner steadiness rather than external solutions. Marcus was dealing with problems he couldn't fully resolve. His writing doesn't focus on fixing the world. It focuses on how to remain grounded while acting within limits that can't be removed.

This book approaches his work with that understanding.

It doesn't treat Marcus Aurelius as someone to admire from a distance or imitate in detail. It treats him as a human being using reflection to stay aligned with his responsibilities, especially when doing so felt difficult.

Reading *Meditations* this way also guards against misunderstanding. If we expect a finished philosophy, we may be frustrated by repetition or lack of structure. If we expect motivation or reassurance, we may miss the point altogether.

The text is better read as a record of practice.

It shows what it looks like to return, again and again, to a small set of principles when circumstances refuse to cooperate. The value isn't in novelty or clever insight. It's in consistency under strain. That approach fits modern life more closely than it may seem.

Many challenges today are ongoing rather than dramatic. Stress doesn't arrive once and leave. It repeats. Decisions return in slightly altered forms. The work of staying balanced is rarely finished, rarely rewarded with a sense of closure.

Marcus wrote to remind himself how to meet those conditions without losing his sense of duty or composure. He wasn't escaping pressure. He was learning how to function within it, day after day, without becoming careless or hardened.

This shapes how the rest of this book proceeds.

The focus here isn't on admiration or historical detail, but on use. The question isn't what Marcus believed in theory, or how consistent he was at all times. The question is how his reflections can help clarify our own responses when we're under pressure.

The goal isn't to turn you into a Stoic by name or identity. There's no lifestyle to adopt, no image to maintain. The aim is simpler than that, and more demanding.

It's to make certain ideas clearer and more available when life feels crowded, demanding, or unclear. Ideas that help steady judgment. Ideas that make responsibility feel manageable rather than overwhelming.

Marcus Aurelius doesn't offer comfort in the form of reassurance.

What he offers is steadiness.

His writing shows how one person tried to remain reasonable, disciplined, and humane while carrying more responsibility than he ever sought—knowing that many outcomes were beyond his control.

Approached this way, *Meditations* becomes less distant and more practical. It reads not as a monument or a manual, but as a working notebook. A place where someone returned, repeatedly, to remind himself how to act when conditions were less than ideal.

That's also how it's meant to be read here.

2

What Stoicism Actually Teaches

Stoicism is often misunderstood before most people ever encounter it.

For some, it suggests emotional coldness. For others, rigid discipline or withdrawal from ordinary life. These impressions usually come from caricature, not from the practice itself, and they obscure what Stoicism was actually concerned with.

At its core, Stoicism is about learning how to meet reality without unnecessary resistance or confusion. It begins from a simple observation.

Some things are up to you.

Most things are not.

This distinction isn't offered as a theory to admire. It's a practical filter for daily life. Without it, attention scatters. Frustration grows. Energy gets spent arguing with conditions that won't change.

Marcus Aurelius returned to this idea repeatedly, not because it was elegant, but because it was difficult to live by. Knowing the difference between what you can influence and what you cannot doesn't remove effort.

It changes where effort goes.

What you can control is limited, but not insignificant. You can shape how you judge events. You can decide how carefully you act. You can choose whether to add resentment, panic, or excess emotion to a situation already demanding enough.

What you cannot control is far more extensive. Outcomes, other people's behavior, timing, chance, recognition—all of this sits outside your authority, whether you accept that or not. Stoicism asks only that you acknowledge this fact, not that you approve of it.

This acknowledgment quietly changes the nature of effort.

Instead of trying to manage everything, attention narrows to what's actually within reach. Decisions become clearer. Responsibility becomes more precise. The goal isn't to avoid difficulty, but to avoid unnecessary friction.

Stoicism also places duty at the center of life.

Not duty as obedience to rules. Not duty as self-sacrifice for approval. Duty here means responding as well as you can to the role you occupy, given the circumstances you're in. Marcus Aurelius didn't imagine a life detached from obligation. He understood himself as embedded in a web of responsibilities he hadn't chosen.

Stoicism doesn't offer escape from this reality. It offers a way to carry it without becoming distorted by it.

Stoic thought doesn't separate inner life from action. Clarity of judgment matters because it affects behavior. Self-command matters because decisions have consequences. Reflection isn't an end in itself—it's a form of maintenance.

A common misunderstanding is that Stoicism teaches indifference.

In practice, it teaches discrimination. It asks you to care deeply about acting well while loosening your grip on how actions are received or rewarded. This balance is difficult. It runs against instinct. That's why Marcus had to remind himself of it so often.

Emotional discipline, in this context, doesn't mean emotional absence.

Anger, fear, disappointment, desire—they still arise. Stoicism doesn't pretend otherwise. What it questions is the automatic authority these reactions are given. Feeling something isn't the same as being obliged to act from it, even when the feeling feels urgent.

Between stimulus and response, there's a brief space. Stoic practice focuses on widening that space just enough to allow judgment to intervene—not to erase emotion, but to prevent it from taking command.

This restraint isn't passive.

It's active and deliberate.

Marcus Aurelius wrote repeatedly about meeting events "as they are," without adding interpretation that inflames them. A setback doesn't need a story about injustice. A delay doesn't need a narrative of disrespect. Often, the first problem is manageable. The second is optional.

Stoicism trains attention toward this difference.

It also insists on realism. There's no expectation that life will become smooth or fair. Difficulty is treated as normal. Change, loss, disappointment—these aren't framed as failures of the system, but as features of existence.

This realism isn't pessimistic.

It's stabilizing, especially over time.

When expectations align more closely with reality, fewer shocks are required to recalibrate them. Energy is conserved. Focus improves. The mind becomes less reactive and more deliberate.

Another misconception is that Stoicism discourages engagement.

In fact, it assumes engagement. Marcus Aurelius didn't withdraw from public life to preserve calm. He sought calm to remain effective within public life. The purpose of inner steadiness wasn't personal comfort—it was functional clarity.

Stoicism values reason, but not abstraction. Reason here means the capacity to pause, assess, and choose proportionately. Practical reason, exercised in ordinary decisions, not a detached intellectual ideal.

Stoic writing often returns to the same themes—not because the ideas are complex, but because they're easy to forget under pressure. The repetition reflects the conditions of use.

Stoicism doesn't promise peace at all times.

It offers orientation instead.

A Common Misunderstanding

Stoicism is often taken to mean emotional distance or personal detachment. In practice, it's almost the opposite.

The Stoic concern isn't how to feel less, but how to respond more clearly.

Emotions aren't denied or argued away. They're noticed, examined, and prevented from taking automatic control.

What Stoicism resists isn't feeling, but confusion—especially the habit of reacting before judgment has had time to intervene.

It helps establish what deserves attention, what deserves effort, and what can be allowed to pass without resistance. It doesn't remove difficulty, but it reduces uncertainty about how to meet it. For modern readers, this is often the most valuable aspect.

Life today places constant demands on attention and judgment. Information arrives faster than it can be evaluated. Expectations multiply. The line between responsibility and overextension is easy to lose.

Stoicism provides a way to redraw that line.

Not by withdrawing. Not by numbing response. But by clarifying priorities. Act where action matters. Accept where acceptance is required. Preserve integrity of judgment even when outcomes remain uncertain.

This chapter isn't meant to provide a complete account of Stoic philosophy. It's meant to establish a working understanding—enough to read Marcus Aurelius without distortion, and enough to see his reflections as tools rather than doctrines.

The chapters that follow will return to these ideas from different angles: control, duty, emotion, perspective. Each explored through Marcus' own words, always with an eye toward use rather than admiration.

Stoicism, as it appears here, isn't an identity to adopt. It's a discipline of attention—a way of meeting life that favors clarity over impulse, responsibility over reaction, steadiness over display.

It asks little in theory.

In practice, it asks more.

And that's why Marcus Aurelius kept writing to himself, again and again, under conditions that rarely made such discipline easy.

PART II

CONTROL: WHAT IS (AND IS NOT) YOURS

3

Control Over Thoughts, Not Events

The first two chapters set the stage—who Marcus was, what he faced, what Stoicism actually means when stripped of caricature. Now we shift from context to practice.

What follows is built around Marcus Aurelius' own reflections. Not maxims to admire or rules to follow—these are working notes, written under pressure, often at the end of difficult days. Each passage serves as a point of orientation, something meant to clarify judgment when it starts to blur.

This chapter focuses on a distinction Marcus returned to more than any other, one he apparently couldn't master once and for all: the difference between what disturbs us and what we *think* disturbs us.

Events themselves are rarely the main source of disturbance. The weight they carry comes from how we interpret them. The same situation can feel manageable or overwhelming depending on the story we tell ourselves—what it means, what it says about us, what it threatens.

Marcus knew this intellectually. But knowing something and living by it are different things. He had to remind himself repeatedly, especially when circumstances made it hardest to remember. When he was exhausted. When people let him down. When outcomes felt unfair and the urge to blame something—anything—became almost irresistible.

The notes that follow reflect that effort: the work of redirecting attention away from events he couldn't control and back toward the one thing he could—his own response.

They focus on learning where your influence actually lies and where it doesn't. Not in abstract terms, but in the specific moments that test this distinction. When frustration spikes. When a situation feels intolerable. When your mind starts spinning and control seems to slip away.

What follows isn't a theory of calm. It's a practice of clarity.

"You have power over your mind—not outside events. Realize this, and you will find strength."

In tua potestate est animus, non externa.

What Marcus Aurelius Meant

There's a boundary here that doesn't move, no matter how much we push against it. Events unfold according to causes beyond any single person's control—other people act as they will, outcomes depend on timing and chance, circumstances shift without consulting us. What remains within reach is narrower, but it's also the only thing that's truly decisive: how your mind responds.

Strength, as Marcus understands it, doesn't come from bending circumstances to your will. It comes from maintaining command over judgment when circumstances refuse to cooperate. Confuse these two domains—trying to control what was never yours to control—and you end up exhausted, burning energy on problems that don't budge. Keep them distinct and something steadier emerges: not power over events, but power over your response to them.

Why This Still Matters

You read an email and your shoulders tense. A meeting gets rescheduled and your whole afternoon feels ruined. Someone's late and you're already writing the story about what it means. Most of what we experience as stress comes from trying to manage results that were never fully ours to manage—chasing approval we can't secure, outcomes we can't guarantee, certainty that doesn't exist.

When this fails, the failure feels personal, like a deficit in ourselves rather than a misunderstanding about where influence actually ends. Remembering this boundary helps effort return to a sustainable scale without removing responsibility—just placing it where you can actually exercise it.

How to Apply This Today

Change the question. Not "How do I fix this entire situation?" but "What response is mine to give?" That shift—from total control to actual responsibility—changes everything. You can't always bend circumstances, but you can choose how you meet them.

"If you are distressed by anything external, the pain is not due to the thing itself, but to your judgment about it—and this you will find you can change."

Si quid externum te angit, non res ipsa est quae te perturbat, sed iudicium tuum.

What Marcus Aurelius Meant

Something happens—someone says something, a plan falls through, a delay occurs. But distress doesn't spring directly from the event. It waits for a judgment to attach itself first. That judgment assigns meaning: *This is unfair. This is dangerous. This proves I'm not good enough. This will ruin everything.*

Once accepted, it colors the entire experience. Marcus isn't claiming events are harmless or that loss doesn't hurt. He's tracing the emotional force back to its source, and the source isn't always where we think it is. Events remain fixed—what happened, happened. But judgments aren't fixed. They can be examined, questioned, softened, set aside entirely.

Why This Still Matters

Judgments form faster than conscious thought. You experience a delay and immediately assume disrespect. You read a message and interpret tone before you've finished the sentence. You face uncertainty and your mind fills it with worst-case scenarios—not as possibilities, but as facts already unfolding.

These instant interpretations amplify tension without improving anything. They explain why a minor inconvenience can ruin a morning, why a single offhand comment can echo for days, why emotional pressure sometimes far exceeds the actual difficulty of what's happening.

How to Apply This Today

Try this the next time irritation or anxiety spikes: pause for five seconds before reacting. What story have you already written about what just happened? What meaning have you assigned without checking whether it's actually true? The story you're telling yourself—not the event—is probably doing most of the damage.

"Choose not to be harmed—and you won't feel harmed. Don't feel harmed—and you haven't been."

Noli te laedi pati, et non laederis.

What Marcus Aurelius Meant

This isn't denial, and it's not about pretending difficulty doesn't exist. Marcus is pointing to consent—showing that harm becomes complete only when we take it fully inside, when we allow it to define our inner state.

An event can register, can be acknowledged as unwelcome or painful, without being granted the power to become an identity wound. When the mind refuses to adopt the event as damage to your core self, its reach stays limited. What remains is the occurrence itself, stripped of the added weight of wounded identity.

Why This Still Matters

How many experiences still hurt not because they're actively happening, but because we keep them alive internally? A remark gets replayed in the shower, during commutes, before sleep. A slight gets remembered, rehearsed, refined into a narrative about what it means about us. Attention keeps returning to the same point of contact—and that repeated engagement, not the original event, sustains the sense of harm.

Some difficulties fade in hours. Others linger for weeks, months, years. Often the difference isn't their objective severity—it's whether we continue to engage with them after they've passed.

How to Apply This Today

Let one problem end where it ended. Not suppress it, not pretend it didn't matter, not convince yourself you're fine when you're not. Just let it be finished. If there's nothing left to do about it, stop doing something about it mentally.

"Such as are your habitual thoughts, such also will be the character of your mind; for the soul becomes dyed with the color of its thoughts."

Quales cogitationes tuae assiduae sunt, talis et animus tuus erit; tingitur enim animus cogitationibus.

What Marcus Aurelius Meant

Marcus isn't talking about positive thinking or changing your mood through affirmations. He's describing a gradual staining process—like fabric absorbing dye. A single thought passes through and leaves almost no trace. But thoughts that return habitually, that show up every morning before you're fully awake, that reappear whenever your attention isn't occupied—those settle into the texture of your mind.

Over time, what you repeatedly think about doesn't just influence how you see things. It becomes how you see things. The patterns harden into character—not because they're true, but because they're familiar. What feels possible, what feels threatening, what feels worth your effort—all of this gets shaped by the thoughts you've allowed to repeat unchallenged.

Why This Still Matters

You're not experiencing reality directly. You're experiencing it through a filter built from habitual thoughts, most of which you didn't consciously choose. "I'm always behind." "People can't be trusted." "Things never work out for me." These aren't observations—they're interpretations that have repeated so often they feel like facts about the world.

Two people walk into the same situation with the same information. One sees opportunity. The other sees risk. The difference isn't in the situation—it's in what their minds have been habitually dwelling on, what patterns have been reinforced through repetition. Your life doesn't just reflect your circumstances. It reflects the mental patterns you've let become permanent.

How to Apply This Today

Notice one thought that shows up regularly without being invited. Not a reaction to something specific—just a background pattern. "I should be further along." "No one really gets it." "This won't last." Don't fight it. Just mark it when it appears. Count how many times it shows up today. That frequency tells you how much of your mental landscape it's already colored.

"Everything we hear is an opinion, not a fact. Everything we see is a perspective, not the truth."

Omnia quae audimus opinio est, non res; omnia quae videmus prospectus est, non veritas.

What Marcus Aurelius Meant

Marcus is drawing a hard line between two layers of experience. There's what actually happens—the raw event, the words spoken, the situation unfolding. Then there's the interpretation we immediately overlay on top of it: what it means, why it happened, what it says about us or them.

We rarely experience the first layer cleanly. By the time we register something, we've already filtered it through assumption, past experience, expectation. Someone says something and we hear not just the words but intent, subtext, judgment. We see an expression and interpret mood, approval, threat. The gap between what's actually there and what we think is there can be enormous, yet we treat our interpretation as if it were the thing itself.

Why This Still Matters

Two people witness the same meeting and leave with completely different accounts of what happened. Not because one is lying, but because each filtered the same events through different frameworks—different concerns, different histories, different expectations about what people mean when they say certain things.

This isn't just about miscommunication. It's about how much of what we react to each day isn't actually real. We're responding to our interpretation of events, our assumption about what someone meant, our projection of where things are heading. The original event—the actual words, the actual expression, the actual situation—often gets lost under layers of opinion we've mistaken for fact.

How to Apply This Today

The next time someone says something that triggers a strong reaction, stop before responding. Ask yourself: "What did they actually say?"—the literal words, nothing added. Then ask: "What story did I immediately attach to those words?" The gap between those two answers shows you how much of your reaction is about interpretation, not reality.

"You always own the option of having no opinion."

In potestate tua est nullam habere opinionem.

What Marcus Aurelius Meant

Not everything requires your judgment. Not every situation demands that you form a position, make a determination, or decide what it means. The mind treats evaluation as automatic—something happens and immediately it begins categorizing, interpreting, assigning significance. But that process isn't mandatory. You can observe something without filing it under good, bad, threatening, or insignificant.

This isn't apathy or withdrawal. It's recognizing that many reactions we treat as inevitable are actually optional. When you suspend judgment—even temporarily—you create space. The event remains visible, but it doesn't hook into your emotional system and start pulling. What stays is the fact itself, without the weight of your verdict attached to it.

Why This Still Matters

We're conditioned to have opinions about everything. News arrives and we're expected to react. Someone shares something and we feel pressure to respond with approval or criticism. Silence gets mistaken for indifference, so we fill it with commentary we haven't actually thought through.

This constant evaluation drains attention. It turns every input into a demand—not just to notice something, but to process it, judge it, integrate it into our worldview. When judgment becomes reflexive rather than deliberate, you lose control over what gets your mental energy. You're reacting to everything instead of choosing what deserves your consideration.

How to Apply This Today

The next time something happens—a comment, a piece of news, a change in plans—resist the urge to immediately decide what it means. Don't form an opinion for ten minutes. Not suppression, not pretending you don't care. Just withholding judgment to see if the situation actually requires one. Most of the time, it doesn't.

"Confine yourself to the present."

Te ipsum intra praesentia contine.

What Marcus Aurelius Meant

This isn't inspirational advice about living in the moment. Marcus is identifying a practical boundary. The present is the only place where your influence actually exists. The past is fixed—you can analyze it, learn from it, regret it, but you can't change what already happened. The future is speculative—you can prepare, anticipate, worry about it, but you can't act in a time that hasn't arrived yet.

When the mind wanders outside the present—replaying what's done, rehearsing what might come—it's spending energy where no actual work can be performed. Confining yourself to the present means keeping attention anchored where judgment can still operate, where decisions can still be made, where effort can still produce results.

Why This Still Matters

Attention rarely stays where it's useful. It drifts backward into regret, forward into anxiety, sideways into speculation. You're sitting in a meeting but mentally replaying an earlier conversation. You're working on a task but worrying about tomorrow's deadline. You're with someone but thinking about the next thing you need to do.

This constant mental displacement creates a strange kind of exhaustion—you're never fully engaged with what's actually happening, so nothing ever feels complete. Tasks take longer because attention keeps leaving. Conversations feel unsatisfying because you're only half-present. The present moment becomes something to get through rather than the only place where your life is actually occurring.

How to Apply This Today

For the next ten minutes, anchor attention to what you're doing right now. Not the whole day, not the next task, not what happened this morning—just this. When your mind moves to past or future, bring it back without judgment. You're not trying to stay present forever. Just proving to yourself that you can, even briefly, and noticing what changes when you do.

4

Letting Go Without Becoming Passive

Letting go is often misunderstood.

For many people, it sounds like giving up. Disengaging. No longer caring about what happens. It's easy to see why—in everyday language, letting go usually signals withdrawal or resignation, especially after effort has failed.

Marcus Aurelius used the phrase differently.

For him, it wasn't about stepping back from responsibility. It was about releasing attachment to outcomes while staying fully committed to action. The distinction matters. Without it, acceptance looks like passivity, and people mistake composure for not caring.

Stoic acceptance doesn't reduce effort—it refines it.

It asks you to stop investing energy in what you can't control so you can act more clearly where action still matters. This isn't indifference to results. It's not detachment from duty. The aim is to act without being distorted by frustration, fear, or resentment—emotions that cloud judgment more than they sharpen it.

Marcus had to learn this balance repeatedly. His notes show someone working to let go of outcomes without abandoning responsibility, discovering that releasing insistence on results didn't weaken his commitment—it steadied it.

The reflections that follow aren't about detachment or surrender. They're about staying grounded where you are without being pulled off balance by what lies beyond your reach.

"Accept the things to which fate binds you, and love the people with whom fate brings you together—but do so with all your heart."

Quae fata tibi dederunt, ea accipe, et eos ama cum quibus te sors coniunxit.

What Marcus Aurelius Meant

You don't get to choose your starting point. Circumstances arrive without consultation. People appear in your life without asking permission. Jobs, family situations, responsibilities—most of what defines your daily reality wasn't selected from a menu of options. Marcus isn't urging resignation here. He's naming a condition that can't be avoided.

Acceptance means acknowledging where you actually stand without resistance or complaint. What follows isn't withdrawal—it's engagement. "With all your heart" isn't sentimental language. It means showing up fully within the conditions you've been given, rather than burning energy wishing they were different.

Why This Still Matters

Before any action even begins, people waste enormous effort fighting the fact of where they stand. Wrong job. Wrong city. Wrong relationship dynamic. Wrong family. That resistance delays engagement and drains whatever energy might have gone toward actually navigating the situation.

Accepting the starting point doesn't lock you in permanently. It just allows movement to begin from somewhere real rather than somewhere imagined. You can't steer from a place you're refusing to occupy.

How to Apply This Today

Name three things about your current situation that are fixed, at least for now. Not judgments about them—just facts. Your job. Where you live. Who's in your family. Starting from acknowledgment instead of argument often reveals options that resentment keeps hidden.

"Do what nature now requires of you. Get straight to it if it is in your power, and do not look around to see if anyone will know."

Quod nunc natura postulat, id fac; si in tua potestate est, ne circumspicias.

What Marcus Aurelius Meant

What does the situation itself require? Not what would be ideal. Not what would get noticed. Not what would earn credit or approval. Just: what needs doing right now, given these specific circumstances?

Marcus is cutting through layers of consideration that usually complicate action. When you release concern for recognition, comparison, future validation—when you stop checking whether anyone's watching—the task becomes simpler. Action anchors to necessity rather than visibility. What matters isn't the audience. It's the alignment between what needs doing and what you actually do.

Why This Still Matters

Hesitation often comes not from confusion about what to do, but from distraction about how it'll appear. Will it get acknowledged? Will it count toward something? Will people understand why you're doing it? These questions compete with the task itself, diffusing effort before it even gets applied.

Returning attention to what's actually required—independent of how it'll be perceived—cuts through that paralysis. The work gets cleaner when it's not performing for anyone.

How to Apply This Today

Think about something you've been putting off. Ask: "What does this situation actually need from me?" Not what response would look best or feel most satisfying—just what's required. Then do that, without announcement. See if acting quietly changes how the task feels.

"Do not waste what remains of your life worrying about other people—unless it affects the common good."

Noli reliquam vitae partem consumere aliena cogitando.

What Marcus Aurelius Meant

Other people matter. But not every thought about them is useful. There's a difference between concern and preoccupation, between care and speculation. Much attention gets lost to wondering what they're thinking, what they meant, whether they noticed, how they're judging you.

Marcus is drawing a boundary around where your mental energy actually goes. Concern for the common good—for shared welfare, for relationships that need tending, for problems that affect others—that's worth your attention. Obsessing over others' opinions of you, imagining their judgments, measuring yourself against their success? That produces nothing except noise.

Why This Still Matters

Social media, workplace dynamics, family systems—they all create constant opportunities to compare, speculate, imagine what others are thinking. You see someone's update and wonder if it's aimed at you. You make a choice and immediately start gaming out how different people will react. Your attention scatters across a dozen imagined perspectives instead of staying with your own.

This doesn't make you more connected. It makes you exhausted. When attention stops serving any actual purpose—when it's not improving relationships or guiding decisions—it's just burning fuel.

How to Apply This Today

For one day, track how often your thoughts turn to what other people might be thinking about you. Not about them generally—about you specifically. Each time it happens, redirect. If there's an actual conversation needed, have it. If not, let the speculation drop.

"The impediment to action advances action. What stands in the way becomes the way."

Impedimentum actioni proficit actio. Quod obstat viae, via fit.

What Marcus Aurelius Meant

The obstacle doesn't stop the action—it redirects it. When something blocks your intended path, that blockage itself becomes the material you work with. Not by forcing through it, not by pretending it doesn't exist, but by letting it reshape your approach.

This isn't optimistic spin on bad circumstances. It's recognition that resistance often reveals better routes than the ones you originally planned. The thing standing in your way forces adaptation, creativity, a different angle. Sometimes that forced adaptation produces better outcomes than the original plan would have.

Marcus isn't saying obstacles are good. He's saying they're workable. You can't remove most of them, but you can use them—not despite their presence, but because of it. The impediment doesn't disappear. It becomes part of the solution.

Why This Still Matters

People treat obstacles as reasons to stop acting. The plan was X, but Y got in the way, so now there's nothing to do but wait or complain. That framing makes obstacles into dead ends rather than redirections.

But most obstacles don't actually prevent action—they prevent the specific action you'd planned. There's usually another move available, one that works with the obstacle rather than against it. Finding that move requires letting go of the original plan while staying committed to the original goal.

How to Apply This Today

Next time something blocks your path, stop treating it as a failure of your plan and start treating it as information. What does this obstacle make possible that wasn't visible before? What route does it suggest that you hadn't considered? The way forward often runs through the obstacle, not around it.

"What happens to everyone—bad and good alike—should not be a cause for surprise or complaint."

Quod omnibus accidit, nec mirum nec querendum est.

What Marcus Aurelius Meant

Difficulty doesn't arrive as moral judgment. Loss, frustration, setbacks—they don't select their targets based on who deserves them. They're part of the common condition, distributed unevenly but inevitably, touching everyone eventually regardless of character or effort.

When hardship is seen as part of how things work rather than as personal insult, something shifts. The urge to protest—*this shouldn't be happening to me*—loses its grip. What remains is the actual task: responding as well as you can to what's in front of you, not arguing with the fact that it appeared.

Why This Still Matters

Added strain often comes not from events themselves but from the sense that those specific events shouldn't have happened to you specifically. That belief creates resentment layered on top of difficulty. You're dealing with the problem and with the injustice of having to deal with the problem.

Recognizing that hardship is broadly shared doesn't diminish the pain. But it does prevent isolation and self-pity from turning manageable difficulty into something heavier than it needs to be.

How to Apply This Today

Next time something goes wrong, notice whether your first reaction includes surprise or indignation—a sense of "this isn't supposed to happen" or "why me?" That response adds weight. Dropping it doesn't solve the problem, but it often makes the problem easier to face directly.

"Be like the rock against which the waves continually break; it stands firm, and the raging of the sea falls still around it."

Ut scopulus, adversus quem fluctus franguntur.

What Marcus Aurelius Meant

The rock doesn't stop the waves. Doesn't fight them. Doesn't move to avoid them or wear itself out resisting their force. It just stays where it is. The waves come, break, recede. The rock remains.

This isn't about emotional hardness or becoming numb. It's about stability—maintaining your position without being pulled into constant reaction. External forces continue. Pressure doesn't disappear. But your inner position holds steady, not because nothing affects you, but because you're not letting every impact knock you off balance.

Why This Still Matters

Reactivity gets rewarded in modern environments. Immediate response is mistaken for engagement, for caring, for being present. But reacting to everything means you're being moved by forces outside yourself rather than acting from your own center.

Over time, constant reaction erodes whatever steadiness you might have built. Learning to remain firm—to let some things break against you without requiring a response—preserves both energy and judgment, especially when the impacts keep coming.

How to Apply This Today

Watch for one moment today when you feel the urge to react immediately to something—a message, a comment, an interruption. Don't react. Just stay still. Not suppression, not pretending nothing happened. Just... not moving yet. Notice whether the wave passes on its own.

"Do not be carried away by imagination; limit yourself to what is happening now."

Ne te trahas imaginationibus; intra praesentia te contine.

What Marcus Aurelius Meant

The mind doesn't wait for events to unfold. It rushes ahead, filling gaps with imagined consequences, projected outcomes, anticipated disasters. This feels like preparation—like responsible thinking, like getting ahead of problems. Usually it's just anxiety dressed up as planning.

Events unfold in sequence, one after another. But attention jumps forward, living through scenarios that haven't happened yet and may never happen. Marcus is calling that movement back. Not denying the future exists, not refusing to prepare.

Just refusing to spend energy living in imagined futures while the present sits unattended.

Why This Still Matters

Most anxiety lives in projected futures rather than current facts. You're not stressed about what's happening right now—you're stressed about what might happen next, what could go wrong, what you'll do if the worst case arrives. The present moment is often manageable. It's the next ten imagined moments that feel crushing.

Limiting concern to what's actually unfolding—not what might unfold—doesn't leave you unprepared. It just stops you from experiencing future problems before they're real, which means you're not solving them twice: once in imagination, once in reality.

How to Apply This Today

When you catch yourself spiraling about what's coming—tomorrow's meeting, next month's deadline, how something might play out—stop and ask: "What's actually happening right now, in this moment?" Not what might happen. What is happening. Stay there for thirty seconds before letting your mind move forward again.

"Leave other people's mistakes where they belong."

Aliena peccata relinque.

What Marcus Aurelius Meant

Someone makes a bad choice. Acts carelessly. Drops the ball. Behaves poorly. That's on them. Their error belongs to them—it's theirs to own, theirs to fix if they choose, theirs to live with. Picking it up and carrying it internally doesn't correct anything. It just means you're now carrying weight that was never yours to carry.

Marcus isn't excusing wrongdoing or suggesting you ignore impact. He's drawing a line around responsibility. What other people do is theirs. What you do with that information—how you respond, what boundaries you set, what you let affect you—that's yours. But their actual error? Leave it with them.

Why This Still Matters

Absorbing frustration on behalf of others—coworkers who don't follow through, family members who keep making the same mistakes, institutions that operate poorly—often feels like responsibility, like caring. But it produces fatigue without producing improvement.

You can acknowledge someone's mistake, respond to its consequences, even try to address it directly. But carrying it emotionally, replaying it mentally, letting it occupy attention long after the moment's passed—that doesn't help them and it doesn't help you. It just keeps you tied to something you can't fix alone.

How to Apply This Today

Notice when irritation about someone else's behavior lingers past the point where you can do anything about it. If there's an action to take—a conversation to have, a boundary to set—take it. If not, practice setting the irritation down. Their mistake. Their weight to carry, not yours.

PART III

DUTY: HOW TO ACT IN THE WORLD

5

Doing What Is Right, Not What Is Easy

Doing what's right is often confused with doing what feels good.

In practice, the two rarely coincide. What feels easiest usually reduces friction in the moment. What's right often increases it—asking for restraint, patience, consistency when shortcuts are available and tempting.

Marcus Aurelius understood this tension well.

For him, right action was a quiet alignment between judgment and conduct. Ease wasn't the measure. Integrity was.

The reflections that follow aren't about heroism or self-denial. They're about choosing coherence over comfort, clarity over convenience. Again and again, Marcus returned to the same question: *What does this situation require of me, if I'm to act well?*

Not: What do I want to do? What would be easiest? What would make this go away fastest? Just: What's the right action here, given these circumstances, independent of whether it's pleasant or rewarded?

Doing what's right doesn't guarantee success. It doesn't promise recognition, appreciation, or even good outcomes. What it guarantees is internal consistency—the ability to look back without having to explain yourself to yourself.

Marcus wrote these notes for moments when the easier option was close at hand. When compromise looked reasonable. When no one would know the difference. When cutting a corner would solve an immediate problem without obvious cost.

Those are exactly the moments these reflections are meant for. Not to inspire effort—effort's already there. To steady it when the ground starts to shift.

"If it is right, do it without hesitation. If it is not, do not do it."

Si rectum est, sine cunctatione fac; si non est, omitte.

What Marcus Aurelius Meant

Hesitation grows in the gap between knowing what's right and acting on it. That gap is where justification lives—where you bargain with yourself, hoping to make a questionable action acceptable or delay a difficult one until it feels easier. Marcus is closing that space.

Once judgment is clear, delay doesn't serve integrity. It serves comfort. Right action doesn't require prolonged debate, perfect conditions, or emotional readiness. It requires decision. The moment you know what's correct, the question shifts from "what should I do?" to "will I do it?"

Why This Still Matters

Overanalysis often disguises avoidance as caution. You circle the same decision for days, generating reasons why now isn't the right time, why you need more information, why the stakes are too high. Meanwhile, what you actually know—that this is the right move, or that it's not—sits underneath all that noise, waiting to be acknowledged.

The longer you wait after clarity arrives, the heavier the decision becomes. Not because it's gotten harder, but because you've spent that time building reasons to delay it.

How to Apply This Today

If you're circling a decision you already understand, ask yourself: Is this hesitation protecting clarity, or protecting comfort? If it's the latter, act. The strain of prolonged indecision often exceeds the strain of the action itself.

"Waste no more time arguing about what a good person should be. Be one."

Noli iam disputare qualis vir bonus sit. Esto.

What Marcus Aurelius Meant

This is Marcus at his sharpest. Reflection has value—it clarifies principles, tests assumptions, helps you understand what matters. But there's a point where reflection becomes a substitute for action, where thinking about goodness replaces actually being good.

The gap between knowing what's right and doing it can be filled endlessly with discussion, refinement, analysis. Marcus is calling that what it is: delay dressed up as preparation. Goodness isn't proven through explanation. It's demonstrated through behavior, quietly, in moments when no one's checking whether you're living up to your stated values.

Why This Still Matters

It's easier to clarify values than to act on them. You can spend years refining your philosophy, your principles, your sense of who you want to be—and never close the gap between that vision and how you actually operate day to day.

That gap creates a particular kind of discomfort. Not the productive kind that pushes you forward, but the kind that comes from knowing you're performing integrity in conversation while compromising it in practice. Acting closes that gap. Discussion, past a certain point, just widens it.

How to Apply This Today

Identify one value you've been talking about—to yourself or others—without fully acting on it. Pick one concrete action, small and specific, that aligns with that value. Do it today. Not to prove something, just to close the gap slightly between what you say matters and what you actually do.

"Do not act as if you were going to live ten thousand years. Death hangs over you. While you live, while it is in your power, be good."

Dum vivis, dum licet, esto bonus.

What Marcus Aurelius Meant

Time feels infinite until it doesn't. We operate as if there's always a later—a better moment to act with integrity, less pressure, clearer conditions. Marcus isn't invoking fear of death. He's pointing out that postponement has a cost: integrity deferred often becomes integrity denied.

"While you live, while it is in your power"—that phrase carries urgency without drama. Right now, you have the ability to act well. Tomorrow that may still be true, but it's not guaranteed. Waiting for ideal conditions usually means waiting indefinitely, because conditions rarely cooperate.

Why This Still Matters

The pattern shows up everywhere: waiting to have the difficult conversation, to set the boundary, to say the true thing instead of the convenient thing. You're waiting for less risk, more certainty, a moment when doing the right thing won't cost as much.

But time is finite whether you acknowledge it or not. The moment to act well isn't coming later under better circumstances. It's here, under these circumstances, or it's not coming at all. Remembering that doesn't create panic—it creates follow-through.

How to Apply This Today

Think of one thing you've been putting off because the timing isn't right. Ask yourself honestly: Am I waiting for better conditions, or am I just waiting? If there's no clear threshold you're waiting to cross, that's your answer. Act now, imperfectly, rather than waiting for a perfect moment that isn't coming.

"Never value anything as beneficial to you if it makes you break your word or lose your self-respect."

Ne quid utile tibi putemus quod fidem aut verecundiam eripiat.

What Marcus Aurelius Meant

Some advantages aren't advantages. They promise relief, progress, protection—but they ask for something in return that can't be replaced by whatever they're offering. A promise bent. A standard softened. Self-respect quietly traded for immediate gain.

Marcus is identifying the line that, once crossed, can't be uncrossed by benefit. Integrity isn't negotiable in pieces. You can't compromise it "just this once" and expect the core to hold. The boundary is absolute: if something asks you to break your word or surrender self-respect, it's not beneficial no matter what it promises.

Why This Still Matters

Pressure presents compromise as practical realism. You're told to be flexible, to work with the situation, to recognize that purity is a luxury you can't afford right now. Sometimes that's true. But often it's an invitation to act in ways that'll require explaining yourself to yourself later.

Those explanations get harder over time. The first compromise feels like an exception. The tenth feels like who you are. A hard boundary—won't break my word, won't surrender self-respect—keeps that progression from starting.

How to Apply This Today

When something feels advantageous, pause before taking it. What's it quietly asking you to give up? Not the obvious cost—the hidden one. If the answer involves your word or your self-respect, the trade isn't worth it regardless of what you'd gain.

"If you have assumed a character suited to yourself, keep to it."

Si personam tibi congruentem sumpseris, serva.

What Marcus Aurelius Meant

Character, for Marcus, isn't something discovered—it's something chosen and then maintained. You decide what kind of person you're going to be—honest, fair, restrained, reliable—and then you hold that decision across changing circumstances.

The temptation is to adjust. Different contexts seem to call for different versions of yourself. With this group, you're one way. In that situation, another. Under pressure, you relax standards. When no one's watching, you let things slide. But character requires continuity. The role you've chosen doesn't get renegotiated based on convenience.

Why This Still Matters

Modern life rewards flexibility, often at the expense of consistency. It becomes easy to operate differently depending on context, audience, or what you can get away with. You're not lying—you're just adapting, being strategic, reading the room.

But that creates internal friction. When behavior shifts too much based on circumstance, you start losing track of who you actually are underneath all the adaptation.

Maintaining a steady character—being the same person in different contexts—reduces that friction, even when it limits your options.

How to Apply This Today

Ask yourself: What kind of person have I already decided to be? Not aspirationally—actually. What character have I assumed? Then check whether a choice you're facing fits that. If it doesn't, that's your answer. Consistency often simplifies decisions that feel complex.

"Do nothing against your conscience, even if external pressures demand it."

Contra conscientiam nihil facias.

What Marcus Aurelius Meant

Pressure is real. Authority makes demands. Expectations arrive from every direction. Compliance often seems easier, safer, more practical than resistance. Marcus acknowledges all of that—and still draws the line at conscience.

Conscience isn't negotiable based on external circumstances. It doesn't adjust for urgency, authority, or consequence. It marks a final boundary: beyond this point, you're acting against what you know to be right. External demands may insist. Conscience doesn't argue back. It just holds the line.

Why This Still Matters

Responsibility today often feels divided. Orders come from above. Expectations are implied. Accountability seems shared across enough people that individual conscience can feel like an inconvenience, like overthinking, like refusing to be a team player.

But responsibility, ultimately, rests inward. You can't outsource moral judgment to circumstance, policy, or someone else's directive. When a situation violates conscience, compliance doesn't distribute the weight—it concentrates it, all on you, afterward.

How to Apply This Today

If a situation feels coercive, check where the discomfort is coming from. Is it risk? Or is it conscience? Risk you can weigh against benefit. Conscience you can't. If it's conscience creating the resistance, that's not a signal to push through—it's a signal to stop.

"What does not make a person worse does not make their life worse."

Quod hominem non deteriorem facit, nec vitam deteriorem facit.

What Marcus Aurelius Meant

Loss comes in different forms. Some losses damage circumstances—you lose a job, a relationship ends, a plan falls apart. Others damage character—you act dishonestly, compromise integrity, betray your own standards. Marcus is making a sharp distinction: only the second kind actually makes life worse.

Circumstances can deteriorate without your life deteriorating, as long as character stays intact. External conditions matter, but they're not the measure of a life. Character is. If you come through difficulty without becoming worse as a person—without losing honesty, fairness, self-respect—then the core of your life remains sound, even if everything around it has changed.

Why This Still Matters

We measure life primarily by comfort, success, momentum—all external conditions. When those falter, the experience feels like decline, like things falling apart. And sometimes they are falling apart, externally.

But Marcus offers a different measure, one that's harder to track but more reliable: Are you worse as a person than you were before this happened? If not—if integrity held, if you didn't compromise yourself to avoid the difficulty—then what's been lost might not be what matters most.

How to Apply This Today

When something goes wrong, ask yourself: Has this actually compromised who I am, or just what I have? If it's only circumstances that changed—not character—then much of what feels lost might matter less than it seems in this moment.

"Do not expect Plato's Republic. Be content to make small progress, and treat even that as no small thing."

Noli exspectare Platonis rem publicam; sed parum profecisse contentus esto.

What Marcus Aurelius Meant

Moral life doesn't get built through sweeping transformation. It advances through small, repeated acts of alignment—doing slightly better today than yesterday, holding a standard under pressure, choosing the harder right thing over the easier wrong thing.

Marcus is tempering expectation deliberately. If you're waiting for dramatic change, for a moment when everything clicks into place and integrity becomes effortless, you'll abandon the work long before that moment arrives. Because it doesn't arrive. What arrives instead—if you stay with it—is modest, incremental progress. And that, Marcus insists, deserves respect.

Why This Still Matters

People abandon right action because it feels insufficient. The gap between where they are and where they think they should be seems too wide to cross through small steps. So they wait for conditions that'll allow bigger leaps—more willpower, less pressure, a clear turning point.

But integrity is built through accumulation, not transformation. Small progress, maintained over time, compounds. Recognizing its value—treating it as meaningful rather than dismissing it as inadequate—is what makes consistency possible when results stay modest.

How to Apply This Today

Look at one area where you're trying to act better. Instead of measuring yourself against the ideal, ask: Did I move even slightly in the right direction today? If yes, that counts. Treating small progress as real progress—not as failure to achieve something bigger—often makes it possible to return tomorrow.

6

Work, Service, and Responsibility

Most people think of work as something they do to get something else—security, status, freedom, the means to live the life they actually want. When work delivers on that promise, it's tolerated. When it doesn't, it's resented.

Marcus Aurelius saw it differently.

For him, work wasn't separate from character. It was one of the primary places where character got tested and expressed—not in dramatic moments, but in ordinary tasks, many of them unglamorous, most of them unseen.

Duty, in his view, wasn't an abstract ideal you aspired to. It was a daily practice carried out in whatever role you occupied, whether you'd chosen that role or not. The question wasn't whether the work felt meaningful. The question was whether you could bring meaning to it through how you approached it.

The reflections that follow aren't about ambition or achievement. They're about contribution—about doing what needs doing because it needs doing, not because it'll be recognized or rewarded.

Service, in this sense, isn't self-erasure. It's alignment. Marcus didn't imagine a meaningful life detached from obligation. He understood himself as part of a larger whole, responsible for playing his part with care and seriousness. Work was where that responsibility became visible, where it stopped being a concept and became action.

These notes aren't about finding purpose through work, as if purpose were something work could deliver if you looked hard enough. They're about bringing purpose to the work already in front of you—the tasks you didn't choose, the roles you inherited, the responsibilities that arrived without asking permission.

That shift, from seeking meaning to creating it, changes everything.

"At dawn, when you struggle to get out of bed, tell yourself: I have to go to work—as a human being."

Ad auroram cum graviter expergiscere, dic tibi: opus humanum ago.

What Marcus Aurelius Meant

Work isn't a favor you're doing for someone else. It's not a sacrifice imposed on you. It's part of what it means to be human—contributing, acting, taking up your role in the world. Marcus is reframing the resistance that shows up every morning when the alarm goes off and you don't want to move.

The urge to see work as an intrusion on your freedom—as something stealing time from your "real life"—creates constant friction. But work is where freedom gets exercised, not where it gets stolen. Through responsibility, not despite it, you participate in something larger than immediate comfort.

Why This Still Matters

The modern relationship with work is often adversarial. Work is what you endure to get to the weekend, to retirement, to the life you actually want to live. That framing turns every workday into a kind of imprisonment, every task into time served.

Seeing work as a human function rather than a personal burden doesn't make difficult work easy. But it removes the layer of resentment that makes everything heavier than it needs to be. The work is still there. The fight against having to do it—that's optional.

How to Apply This Today

Tomorrow morning, before you start resisting the day, try this reframe: "This is what humans do. We work. I'm doing the work assigned to my particular life, in my particular circumstances." Not inspiration—just recognition. See if that shifts anything.

"Do not be disgusted, discouraged, or dissatisfied if you do not always succeed in doing what is right."

Ne fastidias, ne deficias, ne doleas si non omnia recte facias.

What Marcus Aurelius Meant

Imperfection doesn't cancel obligation. Marcus isn't lowering the standard—he's acknowledging that meeting it consistently is hard, maybe impossible. Work done well isn't work done flawlessly. Responsibility doesn't require a perfect record.

The pattern he's addressing is familiar: you fall short, feel disgusted with yourself, disengage to avoid more failure. That cycle compounds the original shortcoming. The solution isn't to feel nothing when you mess up—it's to return anyway, without letting discouragement become an excuse to quit.

Why This Still Matters

People often disengage from demanding work because they equate effort with immediate success. When results disappoint—when the project doesn't work out, when the quality isn't where you wanted it, when you realize you dropped the ball—motivation collapses.

But work that matters is rarely work that succeeds on the first try. If failure disqualifies you from continuing, you'll abandon anything challenging long before you get competent at it. Remembering that duty survives failure makes consistency possible.

How to Apply This Today

After your next setback at work, separate what you intended from what happened. The intention was sound even if the result wasn't. That's enough to keep going. You don't need self-reproach. You don't need motivation. Just return to the work.

"Do your job without whining, without scowling, and without seeking praise."

Sine querela, sine tristicia, sine ambitione age.

What Marcus Aurelius Meant

Complaining doesn't improve performance. Resentment doesn't make work easier. Hunting for recognition doesn't make the task matter more. These are additions—layers you're wrapping around the work itself. Strip them away and what's left is simpler: the task, the doing of it, the completion.

Marcus isn't asking you to love every moment or feel grateful for difficulty. He's pointing out that commentary and emotional performance are separate from the work, and they make it heavier without making it better.

Why This Still Matters

Work and visibility have become entangled. You're not just doing the job—you're performing the doing of it, making sure people see you struggling, announcing your effort, waiting for acknowledgment. Recognition becomes a secondary goal, then sometimes the primary one.

When it doesn't arrive—when your effort goes unnoticed, when someone else gets credit, when the work just disappears into the system—dissatisfaction follows. Separating the work from the applause makes the work itself more bearable, because its value stops depending on whether anyone notices.

How to Apply This Today

Pick one task today and do it without mentioning it to anyone. No announcement beforehand, no report afterward. Just complete it cleanly and let it end there. Notice whether doing work silently changes how it feels.

"What brings no benefit to the hive brings none to the bee."

Quod alveo non prodest, nec apibus prodest.

What Marcus Aurelius Meant

You're not separate from the systems you work within. Individual flourishing isn't something you can secure independently of the larger whole you're part of—your team, your organization, your community, your family. When the hive suffers, the bee suffers, whether the bee recognizes it immediately or not.

This isn't selflessness. It's clear-eyed recognition that personal advantage pursued at the expense of shared good eventually undermines itself. You can't thrive in a degraded system. Work that only serves you stops serving you once the larger structure collapses.

Why This Still Matters

Modern work culture often emphasizes individual gain—your advancement, your leverage, your personal brand, your competitive edge. Over time, when everyone optimizes for themselves without regard for the collective, cooperation erodes and the whole system becomes more fragile.

Remembering that your work exists within something larger doesn't mean sacrificing yourself. It means recognizing that your long-term interests align with the health of the larger structure, not with winning at its expense.

How to Apply This Today

Before making your next work decision, ask: "Does this strengthen or weaken the larger system I'm part of?" Not just "Is this good for me?" but "Does this contribute to something beyond immediate personal benefit?" Let that inform the choice.

"Do what you were made for."

Fac quod ad hoc factus es.

What Marcus Aurelius Meant

This isn't about discovering your special calling or unique purpose. Marcus is pointing to function—the basic responsibilities that come with whatever role you occupy. Parent. Manager. Team member. Citizen. Each role carries inherent duties, whether or not you feel passionate about them.

"What you were made for" is less romantic than it sounds. It's what's required of you given your actual circumstances—not what you wish you were doing, not what you'd be doing in ideal conditions, but what needs doing in the role you actually hold.

Why This Still Matters

Dissatisfaction often comes from measuring your current work against imagined alternatives—better roles, more meaningful positions, work that aligns perfectly with your interests. That comparison diffuses effort and breeds restlessness, because reality never matches the imagined version.

Doing what's required in the role you have—doing it well, with full attention—often brings more stability than chasing the perfect position. Fulfillment follows alignment with actual responsibility, not distinction from everyone else's path.

How to Apply This Today

List the basic responsibilities of your current role—not what you wish they were, what they actually are. Choose one. Do it well today, without comparison to other possibilities. Treat that as sufficient.

"No role is so well suited to philosophy as the one you happen to be in right now."

Nullum munus tam aptum est philosophiae quam id quod nunc geris.

What Marcus Aurelius Meant

The perfect role for practicing integrity doesn't exist somewhere else, in some better position with clearer purpose and fewer frustrations. It's the one you're in. Right now. With all its limitations, complications, and mundane demands.

This isn't consolation for being stuck in the wrong place. It's recognition that every role—regardless of status or significance—provides exactly the friction necessary for character development. The difficulties aren't obstacles to philosophy. They're the material philosophy works with.

You don't need a more important job, a clearer mission, or better circumstances to act well. The role you have, with its specific pressures and particular requirements, gives you everything you need to practice restraint, judgment, fairness, and care. Philosophy doesn't require ideal conditions. It requires actual conditions, which you already have.

Why This Still Matters

People delay acting with full integrity because they're waiting for a role that feels worthy of it. "Once I'm in a position where my work really matters, then I'll be serious about how I do it. Once I have more authority, more resources, more clarity about my purpose—then I'll operate at my best."

But that thinking guarantees you'll never develop the habits that would serve you in that imagined better role. Character develops through practice in whatever circumstances you're actually in, not through waiting for circumstances that justify taking it seriously.

The role you have now—even if it feels temporary, frustrating, or beneath your capabilities—is teaching you exactly what you need to learn. The constraints are showing you where your judgment needs work. The frustrations are revealing where patience breaks down. The routine tasks are testing whether you can maintain care when nobody's watching.

How to Apply This Today

Stop treating your current role as preparation for something better. This is it. This is the actual work. Whatever responsibility you hold right now, approach it as if it's exactly the right place to practice acting well. Because it is.

"Do what is in front of you, following reason, with seriousness, energy, and calm."

Quod praesens est, cum ratione, gravitate, industria, tranquillitate age.

What Marcus Aurelius Meant

Responsibility isn't abstract. It's immediate. The task in front of you—the one you're actually doing right now—deserves full attention. Not distracted attention while you think about the next task, not minimal attention while you resent having to do it. Full attention, guided by clear judgment, approached with care.

Seriousness and calm aren't opposites. You can bring both to the same task—treating it as important without treating it as an emergency. Energy without anxiety. Focus without franticness.

Why This Still Matters

Modern work environments reward busyness more than presence. Moving quickly between tasks, handling multiple things at once, appearing productive—these get valued over actually doing any single thing well. That fragments attention and diminishes quality.

Returning to the immediate task—the one directly in front of you, not the five things competing for attention—restores coherence. Work done with calm, focused energy produces better results than work done in a state of constant reaction.

How to Apply This Today

For the next task you do—even if it's small—give it your complete attention for its entire duration. Not the whole day. Just that one task. No checking email, no mental planning of what's next, no distraction. Just that. Then notice what quality of work emerges when attention doesn't split.

PART IV

INNER CALM IN A DISORDERED WORLD

7

Mastering Emotion Without Denying It

The standard advice about emotions comes in two versions, both wrong.

Either you're told to feel your feelings fully, let them flow, trust your emotional truth, as if emotions were infallible guides that always point toward what's right. Or you're told to suppress them, stay rational, keep emotions out of important decisions, as if feeling something were a sign of weakness that needs to be overcome.

Marcus Aurelius didn't accept either frame.

He didn't believe that feeling less made you better. But he also knew that letting emotion take command led to regret more often than resolution. Making decisions from anger. Acting from fear. Speaking from hurt. These rarely ended well. What concerned him wasn't the presence of emotion, but losing judgment under its weight.

Emotions arise naturally. Fear, anger, disappointment, desire show up without asking permission, often triggered by events you can't control. They signal something: concern, attachment, threat, loss. The question isn't whether to feel them. The question is whether to let them dictate what you do next.

Marcus didn't expect to become calm by nature. He knew he wouldn't. What he worked toward was staying steady by practice—building the ability to feel something intensely without immediately acting from it.

The reflections that follow show how he learned to notice emotion without surrendering to it. Not through repression, not by trying to force feelings down or pretend they aren't there. Through pause. Through creating space between what gets felt and what gets done.

That space is where judgment can operate. Not to eliminate emotion, but to prevent it from being the only thing in command when decisions need making.

"How much more harmful are the consequences of anger than the circumstances that aroused them."

Quanto graviora sunt ea quae ex ira sequuntur quam ea quae iram movent.

What Marcus Aurelius Meant

Anger arrives with a story attached: *This shouldn't have happened. Someone needs to pay. I have to respond now.* That story feels true in the moment, feels justified, feels like the only reasonable reaction to what just occurred.

But Marcus is pointing to what happens next. The thing that made you angry—the comment, the slight, the inconvenience—that's often manageable, often minor, often forgotten by tomorrow. The damage you do while angry? That lasts. Words you can't take back. Decisions made from heat instead of judgment. Relationships strained or broken because you couldn't wait five minutes before reacting.

The original offense rarely matters as much as what you do with the anger it creates.

Why This Still Matters

Anger feels like power in the moment. It feels like you're standing up for yourself, setting boundaries, refusing to be disrespected. And sometimes anger is appropriate—it signals that something matters, that a line's been crossed.

But acting from anger, speaking from anger, deciding from anger—that rarely produces the outcome you actually want. What you get instead is escalation, regret, consequences that outlive the feeling. The person who said something thoughtless moves on. You're still cleaning up what you said back.

How to Apply This Today

Next time anger surges, ask yourself before you act: "Will the consequences of what I'm about to do exceed the problem I'm responding to?" If yes, wait. Even five minutes changes what you're capable of choosing.

"You have the power to strip away many superfluous troubles simply by not adding your own judgments to them."

Multa supervacua mala tollere potes, si nihil eis addas ex opinione.

What Marcus Aurelius Meant

Something happens. That's layer one—the actual event, the thing that occurred. Then your mind gets involved. It adds meaning, interpretation, narrative. *This means they don't respect me. This proves I can't trust anyone. This is going to ruin everything.* Those additions feel like accurate assessments of reality. They're not. They're judgments you're overlaying onto what happened.

Strip away those judgments and what's left is often smaller, more manageable, less catastrophic than it felt when your interpretations were running. The event itself might still be difficult. But difficulty plus your added story about what it means becomes suffering.

Why This Still Matters

Most emotional escalation happens internally, not externally. The thing that upset you stays the same size. Your thoughts about it grow. You replay it, project future consequences, build explanations for why it happened. Each layer of interpretation adds weight.

When you catch yourself spiraling, it's worth asking: "What actually happened, without my story about what it means?" Often the gap between those two things is enormous.

How to Apply This Today

Pick one thing that's bothering you right now. Write down what actually happened in one sentence—just the facts, no interpretation. Then write down everything you've been telling yourself it means. See the difference? That second part is optional.

"When you are angry, pause."

Cum irasceris, subsiste.

What Marcus Aurelius Meant

Marcus isn't debating whether anger is justified or whether the feeling itself is wrong. He's focusing on timing. Anger wants immediate action—it pushes for response now, before the moment passes, before the feeling fades. That momentum is exactly what needs interrupting.

Pausing doesn't mean suppressing. It just means creating space between the surge of feeling and whatever you do next. In that space, judgment can reenter. Not to eliminate the anger, but to keep it from being the only thing driving the decision.

Why This Still Matters

Anger gains power from speed. The faster you move from feeling to action, the less chance there is for anything else to influence what happens. Words get said. Messages get sent. Decisions get locked in. All before the intensity has had time to settle enough for you to consider whether this is really how you want to handle it.

Slowing the moment doesn't deny the emotion. It just prevents the emotion from being the only factor in what you choose to do.

How to Apply This Today

When irritation appears, even a brief pause—literally counting to ten, taking three slow breaths, walking to another room—can be enough to shift what happens next from reactive to deliberate.

"The best revenge is not to be like that."

Optima ultio est non esse similem.

What Marcus Aurelius Meant

Someone acts badly. Treats you poorly. Breaks trust. The immediate urge is to respond in kind—to match their behavior, to show them what it feels like, to make sure they don't get away with it. Marcus is offering a different response: don't become what you're reacting against.

Revenge through imitation means you end up acting like the person who wronged you. You've won nothing. You've just joined them. The real power is refusing to let someone else's behavior determine yours—staying who you are regardless of how they're acting.

Why This Still Matters

When someone treats you badly, the temptation is to mirror it back—to be just as dismissive, just as harsh, just as unfair. "They started it" feels like justification. But lowering yourself to their standard doesn't restore anything. It just means there are now two people acting badly instead of one.

Refusing to mirror the behavior—staying calm when they're hostile, staying fair when they're not, staying measured when they're chaotic—that's harder. It's also more powerful, because it keeps you from becoming someone you'll have to explain to yourself later.

How to Apply This Today

Think of someone who's treated you poorly recently. Instead of planning how to return the favor, ask: "What would it look like to respond without becoming like them?" That question usually reveals a better path than reciprocation.

"Do not be carried away by impressions."

Ne te rapi a phantasiis.

What Marcus Aurelius Meant

Impressions arrive constantly, colored by emotion, shaped by memory, filtered through expectation. You see someone's expression and read hostility. You hear a tone and assume criticism. You notice silence and interpret rejection. These impressions feel like observations, like you're just seeing what's there. But you're not—you're constructing meaning from incomplete information.

Being "carried away" means treating those impressions as if they were facts, as if what you think you're seeing is definitely what's happening. Marcus is calling for examination instead of automatic acceptance. The impression might be accurate. It might be completely wrong. You can't know until you check.

Why This Still Matters

Impressions today arrive faster than ever—messages, headlines, social media posts, workplace dynamics. Each one triggers an immediate interpretation. That person's ignoring you. This news means disaster. That comment was an attack. The interpretations feel obvious, feel true, feel like the only way to read the situation.

But impressions are often incomplete, often distorted, often more about your current state than about what's actually happening. Treating every impression as decisive creates constant emotional turbulence.

How to Apply This Today

When a strong first impression hits, give it five minutes before acting on it. Not to suppress it—just to see if it holds up under slight scrutiny. Ask: "What else could this mean?" Often that question reveals you were jumping to conclusions.

"If you are pained by any external thing, it is not the thing itself that disturbs you, but your judgment about it. And this you have the power to eliminate at any moment."

Si quid externum te cruciat, non id ipsum te vexat, sed tuum de eo iudicium—quod ut extinguas, in potestate tua est.

What Marcus Aurelius Meant

The sequence matters. Something happens first—the event, neutral in itself. Then a judgment forms about what that event means. That judgment generates the emotional response. We experience this as instant, as one unified reaction, but Marcus is breaking it into stages to show where intervention is possible.

You can't control the event—it already happened. You can't directly control the feeling it triggered—emotions don't respond to commands. But the judgment sitting between event and emotion? That's accessible. That can be questioned, adjusted, or withdrawn entirely. Change that and the feeling often changes with it.

Why This Still Matters

People try to control emotions directly and get frustrated when it doesn't work. "Stop being anxious." "Just calm down." "Don't be upset." These commands fail because they're aimed at the wrong target. Emotions follow judgments. If the judgment stays unchanged, the emotion persists.

Working upstream—questioning the interpretation that's generating the feeling—is more effective than trying to wrestle with the feeling itself. Adjust what you're telling yourself about what happened, and the emotional response often adjusts on its own.

How to Apply This Today

When a persistent feeling won't shift, identify the judgment underneath it. "This means I'm failing." "This proves they don't care." "This will never get better." Ask whether that judgment is actually true, or whether it's one possible interpretation among several. Often loosening the judgment loosens the feeling.

"Today I escaped from anxiety. Or no, I discarded it, because it was within me, in my own perceptions—not outside."

Hodie effugi anxietatem. Immo vero, eam abieci, quia in me erat, in perceptionibus meis—non extra.

What Marcus Aurelius Meant

Watch Marcus correct himself in real time. First impulse: "I escaped from anxiety"—as if anxiety were an external threat he managed to get away from, like dodging a falling rock or outrunning danger.

Then the correction: "Or no, I discarded it." The verb changes completely. You don't escape something internal. You discard it. Like throwing out trash. Because that's where anxiety actually lives—not in the situation itself, but in how you're perceiving the situation.

The events are external. The anxiety about those events is internal, constructed through your interpretation, your projections, your story about what's happening and what it means. Marcus caught himself treating anxiety as if it were being done to him from outside. Then he caught the error and corrected it: anxiety exists in his perceptions, which means it's something he can choose to discard.

Why This Still Matters

People treat anxiety as if it's a reasonable response to external circumstances. "Of course I'm anxious—look at what's happening!" The circumstances get blamed for generating the feeling, as if anxiety were a natural consequence that couldn't be avoided.

But circumstances don't create anxiety. Your perception of circumstances creates anxiety. The same event—a presentation, a difficult conversation, an uncertain outcome—produces anxiety in one person and calm focus in another. The difference isn't the event. It's the internal interpretation.

Recognizing anxiety as something you're constructing internally, through how you're perceiving and interpreting, doesn't make it disappear. But it changes the relationship. You're not a victim of external circumstances generating anxiety you can't control. You're hosting anxiety through perceptions you can examine and, if you choose, discard.

How to Apply This Today

Next time anxiety spikes, stop and locate it. Not "what situation is making me anxious?" but "where is the anxiety actually living?" It's not in the email, the meeting, the decision. It's in your thoughts about those things—what they might mean, what could go wrong, how it might turn out. Once you locate it internally, you can discard it the same way you'd discard any other unhelpful thought. Not suppression—discarding. Just: this interpretation isn't serving me, so I'm letting it go.

"Be like the headland against which the waves break and break: it stands firm, and around it the seething of the waters sinks to rest."

Ut promontorium adversus quod fluctus semper illiduntur: stat immotum, et circa ipsum undarum tumultus conquiescit.

What Marcus Aurelius Meant

The headland doesn't stop the waves. Doesn't negotiate with them. Doesn't move to accommodate them or wear itself out resisting. It just stays where it is. The waves come, break, recede. The headland remains. Eventually, around its stability, even the water calms.

This isn't about becoming emotionally numb or detached. It's about maintaining your position when chaos surrounds you—not being pulled into other people's panic, not mirroring their agitation, not letting their emotional state determine yours.

Why This Still Matters

Emotional contagion is real. Tension spreads through teams, families, groups. One person's anxiety triggers another's. Anger escalates as people mirror each other's intensity. Before long, everyone's operating from the same heightened state, and nobody remembers how it started.

Staying measured when others aren't doesn't mean you're disconnected or don't care. It often means you're the only stabilizing force in the situation. Your calm doesn't require theirs. And sometimes your refusal to escalate gives others permission to settle.

How to Apply This Today

Next time you're in a situation where emotions are running high around you, focus on maintaining your own pace of response. Don't match their speed, their volume, their intensity. Stay where you are. See if the situation calms around your stability rather than pulling you into the chaos.

8

Solitude, Reflection, and the Inner Citadel

External conditions rarely cooperate.

Pressure doesn't pause when you need space. Demands don't stop when you need silence. Other people's expectations keep arriving whether you're ready to meet them or not. You can't control when noise stops or when calm arrives. What you can control is whether you build something internal that holds regardless of what's happening around you.

Marcus Aurelius called this the inner citadel.

Not a place you retreat to permanently, but a space you can access even in the middle of chaos. A part of your mind that remains yours, no matter what's being asked of you, no matter who's watching, no matter how much pressure the day is generating.

This wasn't escapism. Marcus wasn't withdrawing from responsibility. He carried more of it than most people ever will. The citadel wasn't about avoiding the world. It was about having somewhere to return to when the world became overwhelming, a place where judgment could steady itself before heading back out.

Solitude, in this sense, doesn't require being alone. It requires internal space, the ability to step back mentally even when you can't step back physically. Reflection isn't something that only happens in perfect conditions. It's something you practice in stolen moments between tasks, in brief pauses before decisions, in the gap between what happens and how you respond.

The reflections that follow aren't about escaping life's demands. They're about building an internal structure strong enough to meet those demands without collapsing under them. Not isolation from the world, but a foundation within yourself that holds steady when everything around you won't.

Marcus built his citadel through writing, through returning to certain ideas repeatedly, through checking his own thinking against principles he'd decided mattered. The practice wasn't dramatic. It was daily, often brief, usually private. But it gave him something external circumstances couldn't take away: a place to stand when standing felt impossible.

"People seek retreats for themselves in the country, by the sea, or in the mountains. You are very much in the habit of yearning for those same things. But this is entirely the trait of a base person, when you can, at any moment, find such a retreat in yourself. For nowhere can you find a more peaceful and less busy retreat than in your own soul."

Homines sibi ipsis refugia quaerunt in agris, in litoribus maris, in montibus. Tu quoque talia vehementer cupis. Sed hoc totum stultissimum est, cum tibi liceat quocumque tempore in te ipsum secedere. Nusquam enim neque quietius neque tranquillus homo secedit quam in animam suam.

What Marcus Aurelius Meant

The impulse is familiar: when pressure builds, you want to get away. A weekend somewhere quiet. A vacation. A complete change of scenery. Somewhere the demands can't reach you, where the noise stops, where you can finally think clearly.

Marcus isn't dismissing that desire. He's pointing out that the retreat you're seeking doesn't require packing a bag. The peace you're looking for exists in a place you already have access to—your own mind. Not metaphorically. Actually. Regardless of where you are physically, regardless of what chaos surrounds you, there's an internal space that can remain yours.

The citadel isn't somewhere you go. It's somewhere you build, through practice, through returning to certain principles, through protecting your attention from being completely colonized by external demands. Once built, it's accessible anywhere, anytime—in the middle of a crisis, during a difficult conversation, between tasks when there's no actual break available.

Why This Still Matters

Modern life doesn't grant much solitude. Open offices, constant connectivity, expectations of immediate response—the environment actively works against having mental space. Waiting for external conditions to provide that space means waiting indefinitely.

But you can create internal space even when external space isn't available. That's not the same as ignoring what's happening around you or pretending pressure doesn't exist. It's building the ability to step back mentally, to access calm judgment, to remember what you actually value—all while still standing in the middle of whatever chaos is demanding your attention.

How to Apply This Today

You don't need a mountaintop. Right now, wherever you are, take sixty seconds. Close your eyes if you can. Breathe deliberately. Let your mind settle away from whatever's pulling at it. That brief internal retreat—that's the citadel. Build the habit of accessing it daily, and it'll be there when you actually need it.

"Look within. Within is the fountain of good, and it will ever bubble up if you will ever dig."

Introrsum aspice; intus est fons boni, qui semper scatere potest, si semper fodies.

What Marcus Aurelius Meant

The search for guidance, for answers, for what to do next—it usually looks outward. Books, mentors, frameworks, other people's opinions. All of that has value. But Marcus is pointing to a source that's often overlooked: your own judgment, when you actually give it space to operate.

"Digging" means doing the work of reflection, of sitting with a problem long enough to let your own thinking develop instead of immediately reaching for someone else's answer. The fountain doesn't produce instant solutions. It requires effort—the effort of thinking things through, of examining your own assumptions, of letting clarity emerge from confusion through actual reflection.

Why This Still Matters

External input is endless and instant. You can google anything, poll your network, find an expert opinion within minutes. That creates a habit of outsourcing judgment before you've done your own thinking. You skip the hard work of figuring out what you actually believe, what actually fits your situation, what makes sense given your specific circumstances.

The fountain dries up when you stop digging—when reflection becomes something you only do after you've already consumed everyone else's thoughts. Maintaining access to your own judgment requires protecting time to think without input, to process without immediate answers, to let your mind work on problems in the background.

How to Apply This Today

Before reaching for external input on your next decision, spend twenty minutes just thinking. No phone, no research, no asking anyone. Just you and the problem. Write if it helps. Walk if movement clarifies. See what emerges before you go looking for answers elsewhere.

"Withdraw into yourself as far as you can."

In te ipsum recede quantum potes.

What Marcus Aurelius Meant

This isn't a call for permanent isolation. Marcus held the most public role imaginable—he couldn't withdraw from the world even if he wanted to. What he's describing is a practice, a temporary movement inward that creates distance from the constant pull of external demands.

"As far as you can" acknowledges limits. You might only get five minutes. You might only manage a few seconds of internal space before the next interruption arrives. That's fine. The practice isn't about achieving perfect solitude—it's about creating whatever degree of internal separation is possible given your actual circumstances.

Why This Still Matters

You're expected to be available constantly. To respond immediately. To stay engaged with multiple channels simultaneously. That expectation makes internal withdrawal feel like failure, like you're not keeping up, like you're letting people down.

But without periodic withdrawal, judgment degrades. Decision quality drops. You start operating purely from reaction instead of intention. The withdrawal isn't escapism—it's maintenance. You're not abandoning responsibility. You're preserving the capacity to meet it well.

How to Apply This Today

Set a timer for five minutes. Step away from every input source—email, messages, people, tasks. Not to think productively, not to solve problems. Just to withdraw. Let your mind settle. Do this once today. That small practice of deliberately stepping back builds the skill you'll need when stepping back isn't optional.

"The things which are external to my mind have no relation at all to my mind."

Ea quae extra mentem meam sunt, nihil ad mentem meam pertinent.

What Marcus Aurelius Meant

External events can affect your circumstances. They can change what you have, where you are, what resources are available. But they can't touch the core of your mind—your ability to judge, to choose how to respond, to maintain your principles—unless you grant them that access.

This sounds like denial until you test it. Someone insults you—that's external. The words exist outside your mind. Whether those words damage your self-respect, change your self-perception, or influence how you see yourself? That happens internally, and only if you allow it. The external event can't force that internal response. It can trigger it, but the permission is yours.

Why This Still Matters

People talk about events "making them" feel or think certain ways. "That ruined my day." "They made me so angry." "This destroyed my confidence." But the event itself doesn't have that power. What has power is your response to the event, which happens internally and remains, ultimately, within your control.

Recognizing this doesn't eliminate difficulty. External events can still be genuinely hard, genuinely unjust, genuinely painful. But they can't reach your mind's integrity unless you open the door. That boundary—between what happens outside and what you allow to happen inside—is the foundation of the citadel.

How to Apply This Today

Next time something external bothers you, pause and identify: What's the external event? What's my internal response? Where's the boundary between them? That distinction shows you where your actual control lives—not over the event, but over whether it gets to define your internal state.

"Remember that your ruling faculty becomes invincible when it rallies and relies on itself, so that it won't do anything contrary to its own will, even if its position is irrational. How much more invincible if its judgment is based on reason and circumspection!"

Memento regendi vim tuam invictam fieri, cum in se colligatur et sibi ipsi fidit, ut nihil contra voluntatem suam faciat, etiam si irrationabiliter stet. Quanto magis si ratione et circumspectione iudicet!

What Marcus Aurelius Meant

The ruling faculty—the part of your mind that makes decisions, forms judgments, chooses how to respond—becomes invincible when it stops looking outside itself for permission or validation. Not invincible in the sense that nothing can touch you, but invincible in the sense that nothing can make you act against your own judgment.

Even if your position is wrong, even if your reasoning is flawed, when you operate from genuine internal conviction rather than external pressure, you maintain integrity. And when that conviction is actually based on sound reasoning, on careful thought? Then you're operating from the strongest possible position.

Why This Still Matters

Most decisions get made under pressure from outside: what others expect, what will look good, what avoids conflict, what's easiest to justify. That creates decisions you have to explain to yourself later, choices that don't quite sit right because they weren't really yours—they were compromises with external demands.

The citadel holds when your decisions come from internal deliberation rather than external pressure. Not isolated from reality, not ignoring consequences—but grounded in your own reasoned judgment rather than shaped entirely by what surrounds you.

How to Apply This Today

Face your next significant decision by asking: "What would I choose if no one else's opinion mattered, if there were no external pressure, if I were answerable only to my own judgment?" That answer might not be what you ultimately do—external factors matter—but knowing what your actual judgment is gives you a foundation everything else has to negotiate with, not override.

"A little flesh, a little breath, and a Reason to rule all—that is myself."

Corpusculum, spiritus, mens dirigens—hoc sum ego.

What Marcus Aurelius Meant

Marcus is identifying with the thing that can't be taken from him. The body fails, gets injured, ages, dies. Breath comes and goes, will eventually stop. But the reasoning faculty—the part that observes, judges, chooses—that remains yours as long as you're conscious.

This isn't denying physical reality or pretending the body doesn't matter. It's locating your essential self in the only part that can't be controlled by external force. Someone can imprison your body, restrict your movements, control your physical circumstances. But they can't make you think what they want you to think, judge as they want you to judge, value what they want you to value. That remains sovereign.

Why This Still Matters

Identity gets wrapped up in things that can be taken away: appearance, status, possessions, roles, health. When those things change—and they will—people feel like they've lost themselves. But if you identify with the reasoning faculty, with the part that observes and chooses, that remains constant through all external changes.

This is the ultimate citadel: knowing that regardless of what happens to circumstances, body, or external conditions, the core of who you are—your capacity for judgment and choice—remains intact and accessible.

How to Apply This Today

When external conditions feel crushing, when it seems like everything's being taken away, check: Can you still think? Can you still choose how to respond? Can you still maintain your principles? If yes, then the most important part of you is still intact. Everything else is negotiable.

"The mind cannot be forced from outside; the harm is that a person does to themselves."

Mens externa cogi non potest; malum quod sibi ipsi homo facit.

What Marcus Aurelius Meant

External pressure is real. Threats, demands, expectations, consequences—all of that exists and can be intense. But none of it can force your mind to think something, believe something, or surrender its judgment. The mind yields only from the inside, only with your consent.

When harm occurs internally—when peace gets disrupted, when judgment gets clouded, when integrity gets compromised—that's not being done to you by external circumstances. That's something you're allowing to happen through how you're responding to those circumstances. Marcus isn't blaming victims here. He's identifying where actual power lives: not in preventing external pressure, but in how you meet it internally.

Why This Still Matters

People feel helpless when external conditions are bad, as if their internal state must mirror external chaos. But internal state and external circumstances aren't locked together. You can maintain internal calm in external chaos, maintain clear judgment under pressure, maintain your principles when everything around you is compromised.

The harm that destroys the citadel—confusion, panic, loss of judgment—comes from abandoning the internal position, not from the intensity of external attack. The citadel falls from within, not from without.

How to Apply This Today

Under your next wave of external pressure, notice where you're responding by abandoning your internal position—rushing judgment, reacting from panic, compromising principles to reduce immediate stress. Those are the moments when you're doing the harm to yourself that external circumstances can't do on their own. Hold the internal position. Let external pressure exist without surrendering internally to it.

PART V

TIME, MORTALITY, AND PERSPECTIVE

9

Remembering How Brief Life Is

You're going to die.

Not eventually, in some distant abstract future. Actually die. Stop existing. Everything you're worried about, everything you're working toward, everyone you know—all of it ends. For you, specifically, in a timeframe that's shorter than you're pretending it is.

Marcus Aurelius didn't dwell on this to be morbid. He returned to it because forgetting it made him waste time on things that didn't matter. Remembering it clarified what did.

The awareness of death isn't meant to create panic or despair. It's meant to create proportion. When you remember that time is genuinely limited, that you don't get infinite chances to act well or say what needs saying or do what actually matters, certain decisions become simpler. Not easier. Simpler.

What you've been putting off stops being something you'll get to later. Later isn't guaranteed. The conversation you've been avoiding, the work you've been delaying, the relationship you've been taking for granted—these don't wait for you to feel ready. They exist now, or they won't exist at all.

Marcus used mortality as a practical tool, not a philosophical abstraction. Remembering that his time was finite helped him stop wasting it on trivial concerns, pointless conflicts, and the endless postponement of things that genuinely deserved attention. It made the present moment more vivid because it was all he actually had.

This isn't about living every day as if it's your last. That's exhausting and impractical. It's about living every day with the awareness that it might be, which changes what you're willing to let slide, what you're willing to accept as good enough, what you're willing to leave undone.

The reflections that follow use mortality as Marcus did: not to frighten, but to focus. Not to make life feel smaller, but to make what matters feel clearer. They're reminders that time keeps moving whether you're using it well or wasting it, and that the choice between those two is happening right now, not someday.

"You could leave life right now. Let that determine what you do and say and think."

Exire e vita iam potes. Id te facere, dicere, cogitare determinet.

What Marcus Aurelius Meant

This isn't a reminder that you might die someday in the distant future. It's a reminder that you could die today. Right now. In the next hour. Without warning, without time to prepare, without getting to finish what you started.

That sounds grim until you sit with what it actually does: it clarifies. When you remember that this conversation might be your last with this person, that this task might be the last work you do, that this decision might be the final one you make—posturing drops away. What you'd normally waste time on suddenly seems absurd.

Marcus isn't asking you to live in fear of death. He's asking you to let death's presence shape how you operate while alive. What would you say if you knew these were your last words? How would you treat someone if this were your last interaction? What would you focus on if today were all you had?

Why This Still Matters

Most of life gets lived as if there's infinite time to fix things later, to say what needs saying eventually, to get serious about what matters once conditions improve. That assumption—that later is guaranteed—creates a kind of casual negligence. Important things get postponed. Relationships get taken for granted. Work that matters waits for a better moment.

Remembering you could leave life right now doesn't make you live in panic. It makes you stop treating the present like a dress rehearsal for some future performance. This is it. This is the actual life, happening now.

How to Apply This Today

Before your next significant interaction or decision, pause and ask: "If this were the last time, would I do this differently?" Not to create pressure, but to cut through whatever story you're telling yourself about why good enough is acceptable for now. Often that question reveals you already know what actually deserves your attention.

"Think of yourself as dead. You have lived your life. Now take what's left and live it properly."

Te mortuum esse cogita. Vitam vixisti. Quod superest, recte vive.

What Marcus Aurelius Meant

Imagine you've already died. Everything you've done up to this moment—that's complete, finished, unchangeable. All your mistakes, all your successes, all the time you wasted or used well—that's done. You can't go back and fix it. You can't improve it. It's over.

Now imagine you've been given a second chance. Whatever time remains—whether it's fifty years or fifty minutes—that's bonus time. Time you didn't earn, time you aren't owed, time that could end at any moment. How would you use it?

Marcus is using this thought experiment to create freedom. When the past is treated as already complete, you stop carrying its weight. When the future is treated as borrowed time, you stop wasting it. What remains is just this: what are you going to do with what's left?

Why This Still Matters

People carry their past failures as if those mistakes are still actively happening, as if there's still time to go back and do better. That backward focus consumes energy that could go toward acting better now. Similarly, treating the future as infinite creates permission to postpone—to live carelessly today because there's always tomorrow to get serious.

Treating yourself as already dead, as living on bonus time, changes the calculation. The question isn't "How do I make up for what I got wrong?" It's "What do I do with what's left?" That shift often releases you to act with more care and less burden.

How to Apply This Today

Today, act as if everything before this moment is finished—unchangeable, complete, no longer your responsibility to fix. What you do from this point forward is the only thing you can influence. Knowing that, what deserves your attention right now?

"It is not death that a man should fear, but he should fear never beginning to live."

Non mors timenda est, sed ne umquam vivere incipias.

What Marcus Aurelius Meant

Most people aren't afraid they'll die. They're afraid they'll die without having actually lived—without having done the work that mattered, built the relationships that deserved care, said the things that needed saying, become the person they were capable of being.

The fear isn't death itself. It's reaching the end and realizing you spent your entire life preparing, postponing, waiting for the right conditions—and never actually began. Never risked enough to fail. Never cared enough to be hurt. Never committed enough to be disappointed. You stayed safe, stayed comfortable, stayed in waiting mode. And then time ran out.

Marcus is saying the real danger isn't that life ends. It's that it ends before it ever really starts—before you stop rehearsing and actually show up, before you stop planning and actually act, before you stop protecting yourself and actually live.

Why This Still Matters

It's easy to spend years in preparation mode. Getting ready to start the real work. Waiting until you're more qualified, more certain, less afraid. Planning to take relationships seriously once things settle down. Intending to live according to your values once the pressure eases.

But the pressure doesn't ease. Certainty doesn't arrive. The perfect conditions never materialize. And at some point, if you're not careful, you realize you've been getting ready to live instead of actually living. The tragedy isn't dying. It's dying without ever having begun.

How to Apply This Today

Identify one thing you've been preparing for, planning for, waiting for the right time to begin. Ask honestly: "Am I actually going to start this, or am I using preparation as a way to avoid starting?" If it's the latter, stop preparing. Begin. Even badly. Even scared. Just begin.

"How small a part of the boundless and unfathomable time is assigned to each of us—and how swiftly it vanishes into eternity."

Quam parva pars temporis infiniti unicuique assignatur—et quam cito in aeternitatem evanescit.

What Marcus Aurelius Meant

Put your life against the timeline of the universe. Billions of years before you existed. Billions of years after you're gone. Your entire life—even if you live to be a hundred—is a microscopic sliver of that vastness. And within that already tiny sliver, how much time do you actually have where you're aware, capable, able to act?

Childhood passes before you understand what's happening. Old age arrives before you're ready. What's left is a brief window where you can actually do something meaningful. And that window is closing whether you're using it well or wasting it.

Marcus isn't trying to make life feel insignificant. He's trying to make you stop treating time as if it's infinite. It's not. It's vanishingly brief. And most of it is already gone.

Why This Still Matters

When time feels infinite, everything can wait. That difficult conversation? Later. That meaningful work? Eventually. That relationship that needs attention? We'll get to it. The assumption that there's always more time creates a casual approach to the time you actually have.

Remembering how brief your portion is—how swiftly it's passing—doesn't create panic. It creates urgency of the useful kind: the recognition that what you're going to do, you need to do now, because later might not come.

How to Apply This Today

Calculate, roughly, how much time you've already used. If you're forty, and you live to eighty, you've got maybe 350,000 waking hours left. Sounds like a lot until you realize you just spent one of them reading this. How many more are you willing to spend on things that don't actually matter?

"Soon you will have forgotten everything; soon everything will have forgotten you."

Cito omnia oblivisceris, cito omnia te obliviscentur.

What Marcus Aurelius Meant

Two movements happening simultaneously: you forgetting everything, and everything forgetting you.

First movement: whatever you're worried about right now, whatever feels permanently significant, whatever mistake feels like it'll define you forever—you're going to forget most of it. The slight you received, the recognition you didn't get, the moment you embarrassed yourself—in five years, you won't remember it clearly. In ten, it'll be gone completely.

Second movement: whatever legacy you're trying to build, whatever reputation you're protecting, whatever impact you're hoping to leave—it won't last. The people who remember you will die. The things you built will decay or be replaced. Within a few generations, even your name will be forgotten. As if you never existed.

Marcus isn't being nihilistic. He's releasing you from the weight of permanence. You don't have to perform for eternity. You just have to act well now.

Why This Still Matters

People exhaust themselves trying to secure lasting significance. Building a legacy. Making a mark. Ensuring they'll be remembered. That pursuit creates pressure that often distorts the very work it's meant to motivate. You stop doing what's right and start doing what's impressive. You stop serving the actual task and start serving your future reputation.

But you won't be around to enjoy that reputation. And it won't last anyway. Remembering that—really internalizing it—can be freeing. It lets you focus on doing good work today without needing it to echo forever.

How to Apply This Today

Think about something you're doing primarily for recognition, for legacy, for how it'll make you look. Ask: "If no one would ever know I did this, would I still do it?" If the answer is no, you might be working for the wrong reason. If yes, then do it well and let the recognition question take care of itself.

"Live as though you were already at the end of life. The time you have left is a bonus."

Tam vive quasi iam ad finem perveneris. Tempus quod superest donum est.

What Marcus Aurelius Meant

Imagine you're ninety years old, looking back at your life. What you've done is done. The choices you made, made. The relationships you built or neglected, built or neglected. You're at the end, and whatever regrets you have, you have to live with them because there's no time left to fix them.

Now step back into your actual age. However old you are, whatever time you have left—that's not owed to you. That's a gift. Bonus time. Time you could easily not have gotten. Use it like someone who knows it's borrowed and could be recalled at any moment.

Marcus is creating a mental position that makes waste harder to justify. When you operate as if you're at the end looking back, trivialities reveal themselves. Things you thought mattered show themselves as distractions. What actually deserves attention becomes obvious.

Why This Still Matters

Most people live as if they're in the middle of an infinite timeline, with unlimited opportunities to get things right later. That creates a kind of sloppiness—casual with time, casual with relationships, casual with effort. "I'll do better next time" becomes the default response to mediocrity.

Living as if you're at the end, as if what's left is bonus time, makes "next time" feel less guaranteed. It doesn't create panic. It creates precision. You become more deliberate about what deserves your remaining time and what doesn't.

How to Apply This Today

At the end of today, imagine you're looking back at how you spent it. What will you wish you'd done differently? What will feel like it mattered, and what will feel like waste? You still have hours left today. Adjust accordingly.

"Remember how many doctors died after furrowing their brows over the sick, how many astrologers after predicting with great pretensions the deaths of others, how many philosophers after endless disquisitions on death or immortality."

Memento quot medici mortui sunt post multas aegrotorum curas, quot astrologi post mortes aliorum magna cum arrogantia praedictas.

What Marcus Aurelius Meant

Doctors who spent their lives studying disease—dead. Astrologers who predicted everyone else's death with great confidence—dead. Philosophers who wrote elaborate theories about immortality—dead. The expertise didn't save them. The knowledge didn't protect them. The pretension didn't matter. Death came anyway.

Marcus is stripping away the illusion that any amount of achievement, knowledge, or status creates exemption. It doesn't. The person who built empires and the person who swept floors both end up dead. The brilliant theorist and the completely ordinary worker—same outcome.

This isn't meant to discourage achievement. It's meant to prevent you from thinking achievement makes you special in the only way that would actually matter: immune to mortality. You're not. No one is. Act accordingly.

Why This Still Matters

Success creates a dangerous sense of exception. People start to feel that their accomplishments, their intelligence, their importance somehow sets them apart from ordinary human limits. That they have more time because they've earned it, because they're doing important work, because they're too valuable to lose.

But mortality doesn't care about your resume. It doesn't check your credentials. The most accomplished person you know will die. The most ordinary person you know will die. You will die. Remembering that levels the playing field and removes the pretension that makes life heavier than it needs to be.

How to Apply This Today

List your accomplishments, your credentials, everything that makes you feel important or special. Now remember: none of it creates exception from death. Given that, what actually matters? Usually the answer is simpler and more human than the achievements suggest.

10

Ego, Legacy, and Letting Go of Recognition

You want to be seen.

Not just noticed, but recognized. Acknowledged for your work. Appreciated for your effort. Remembered after you're gone. It's not vanity—or not entirely. It's human. The desire to matter, to leave a mark, to have your existence registered as significant by someone other than yourself.

Marcus Aurelius felt this too. He was an emperor. Recognition came automatically, built into the role. And yet his private notes reveal someone constantly working against the pull of ego, the seduction of legacy, the temptation to measure his worth by how others perceived him.

The pull is real because it promises something evolution wired us to want: social proof that we matter. But the promise is false. External recognition never delivers what it seems to offer. It doesn't make you more valuable. It doesn't prove you were worth the space you took up. It doesn't secure your significance.

What it does is make you dependent. Dependent on others' opinions to feel good about your work. Dependent on visibility to feel like effort was worthwhile. Dependent on legacy to feel like your life meant something. That dependency distorts everything: what you choose to work on, how you treat people, what you're willing to compromise to maintain the image you've built.

Marcus saw this trap clearly, probably because he lived inside it. When you're emperor, everything you do gets noticed, recorded, analyzed. Every decision becomes part of your legacy whether you want it to or not. That kind of constant visibility could have consumed him. Instead, he used it to practice something harder: acting well regardless of who was watching, doing what was right independent of whether anyone would remember.

The reflections that follow aren't about becoming humble or learning to accept obscurity. They're about freedom—the freedom that comes from doing good work without needing applause, from acting with integrity without needing witnesses, from building something worthwhile without needing it to outlast you.

Marcus wrote these notes for himself, in private, with no expectation they'd ever be read. The irony is that this private writing is what survived. The public performances, the imperial decrees, the carefully managed image—most of that's forgotten. What lasted was the work he did when no one was watching, the thoughts he recorded without concern for how they'd make him look.

That's the paradox at the heart of this chapter: the things you do for recognition rarely earn it. The things you do without needing it often matter more. Not because the universe rewards humility, but because work done without the distortion of ego tends to be better, clearer, more honest work.

"Ambition means tying your well-being to what other people say or do. Self-indulgence means tying it to the things that happen to you. Sanity means tying it to your own actions."

Ambitio est obligare animum ad aliorum dicta aut facta. Luxuria est obligare ad ea quae tibi accidunt. Sanitas est obligare ad tua facta.

What Marcus Aurelius Meant

Three ways to measure yourself, three different dependencies. Ambition ties your sense of worth to external judgment—whether people praise you, recognize you, approve of what you've done. Self-indulgence ties it to circumstances—whether you're comfortable, whether things are going your way, whether you're getting what you want.

Sanity, as Marcus defines it, ties well-being to the only thing actually within your control: your own actions. Not how those actions are received. Not whether they succeed. Just whether you acted well—with integrity, with care, with alignment to what you know is right.

The first two create instability because they depend on things you can't control. People's opinions shift. Circumstances change. Comfort comes and goes. If your well-being is tied to any of that, you're constantly at the mercy of forces outside yourself. Only the third option creates stability, because it depends solely on what you choose to do.

Why This Still Matters

Most people operate from the first position without realizing it. They feel good when praised and terrible when criticized. They measure the value of their work by how it's received rather than by whether they did it well. Success means recognition. Failure means being ignored.

That creates a exhausting dependence on external validation. You're not working for the work itself anymore—you're working for the response. And when the response doesn't come, or comes in the wrong form, the work feels meaningless even if it was solid.

Tying well-being to your own actions instead doesn't mean ignoring feedback or operating in isolation. It means your fundamental sense of worth comes from whether you acted with integrity, not from whether anyone noticed or cared.

How to Apply This Today

After your next piece of work, check where your satisfaction is coming from. Is it from knowing you did it well, or from waiting to see how others respond? If it's the latter, practice finding the satisfaction in the doing itself. The work was good or it wasn't, independent of who notices.

"All is ephemeral—fame and the famous as well."

Omnia ephemera sunt—et fama et qui fama celebrantur.

What Marcus Aurelius Meant

Fame doesn't last. The people who achieve it don't last. The people who remember them don't last. Everything dissolves given enough time. The celebrity, the admirer, the memory itself—all temporary, all heading toward the same oblivion.

Marcus isn't being grim. He's being precise. If you're working to be famous, working to be remembered, working to secure lasting recognition, you're working toward something that fundamentally cannot be secured. It's not just that it's hard to achieve. It's that even if you achieve it, it won't last. Eventually, inevitably, it fades.

Why This Still Matters

Legacy has become a cultural obsession. Building something that lasts. Making your mark. Ensuring you're remembered. That drive can produce good work, but it can also distort work—making you chase visibility over substance, impression over integrity, scale over actual quality.

Remembering that fame is ephemeral doesn't mean your work doesn't matter. It means the work matters for what it is and what it does now, not for whether it echoes into some imagined future. The person it helps today is real. The legacy you imagine is not.

How to Apply This Today

Think about work you're doing primarily because you hope it'll make you remembered. Ask: "If this disappeared completely after I'm gone, would it still be worth doing?" If yes, you're working for the right reasons. If no, you might be chasing something that won't satisfy even if you catch it.

"Soon you'll be ashes or bones. A mere name at most—and even that is just a sound, an echo. The things we prize in life are empty, rotten, trivial."

Brevi cinis aut ossa eris. Nomen tantum—et id ipsum sonus est, echo. Quae in vita colimus, vana, putida, parva sunt.

What Marcus Aurelius Meant

Strip away everything that feels permanent and here's what's left: physical remains that nobody wants to look at. Maybe your name gets mentioned a few times after you're gone. But even that—what is a name? Just a sound people make with their mouths. An echo that fades.

The things we spend our lives pursuing—status, recognition, the feeling of being important—these aren't just impermanent. They're hollow. They promise significance and deliver noise. We treat them as if they're the point of existence, and Marcus is saying they're not even real in any meaningful sense.

This isn't nihilism. It's perspective correction. If you can see clearly that most of what you're chasing is empty, you can stop chasing it and focus on what isn't.

Why This Still Matters

People structure their entire lives around things that, examined closely, turn out to be empty. The need to be admired. The need to have your name known. The need to feel important in other people's estimation. These feel urgent, feel necessary, feel like they matter profoundly.

But they're sounds and echoes. Temporary recognition from temporary people about temporary accomplishments. Treating that as the goal distorts everything—how you work, how you treat people, what you're willing to compromise.

Seeing it clearly as empty doesn't make life meaningless. It makes the things that aren't empty stand out more clearly.

How to Apply This Today

List what you're currently treating as important. Then ask for each item: "Is this substance or is this sound?" Recognition is sound. Good work is substance. Reputation is sound. Acting with integrity is substance. Sort accordingly.

"Alexander the Great and his mule driver both died and the same thing happened to both. Either they were taken up into the creative force of the universe, or they were scattered into atoms."

Alexander Magnus et mulio eius ambo mortui sunt, et idem utrique accidit. Aut in vim creatricem universi recepti sunt, aut in atomos dissipati.

What Marcus Aurelius Meant

One person conquered the known world. The other hauled baggage. One's name is still remembered two thousand years later. The other's name was probably forgotten within a generation. And yet, at death, the exact same thing happened to both of them.

Their atoms scattered or returned to the universe or whatever actually happens—Marcus doesn't claim to know. But whatever it is, it happened identically to the emperor and the servant. Achievement didn't create exemption. Fame didn't alter the outcome. They both ended up in the same place.

Why This Still Matters

We operate as if achievement creates fundamental difference, as if success elevates you to a different category of human. The person who builds something important, who achieves recognition, who makes their mark—surely they're different from someone who lives an ordinary life and dies unknown.

But they're not. Not where it actually matters. Death equalizes completely. The most accomplished person you know will die. The least accomplished will die. You will die. And whatever happens after that, it'll be the same regardless of what you achieved before it.

That doesn't make achievement meaningless. It makes it right-sized. It's meaningful while you're alive to do it and while it helps others. It's not meaningful as an insurance policy against oblivion, because that insurance doesn't exist.

How to Apply This Today

When you catch yourself using achievement as a way to feel fundamentally different from or better than others, remember: Alexander and the mule driver. Same ending. That thought doesn't diminish your work—it just removes the pretension from it.

"What is your vocation? To be good."

Quid est ars tua? Bonum esse.

What Marcus Aurelius Meant

Not "to be famous." Not "to be successful." Not "to be recognized as talented." Just: to be good. To act with integrity. To treat people fairly. To do your work with care. To show up with honesty. That's the vocation. That's what you're here for.

Everything else—the recognition, the achievement, the legacy—those are side effects at best, distractions at worst. They're not the point. Being good is the point. And unlike fame or success, that's completely within your control. You can be good today, right now, in whatever circumstances you're actually in.

Why This Still Matters

People treat their vocation as something complex: building a career, making an impact, leaving a legacy, becoming known for something. Those pursuits create pressure and confusion because they depend on factors outside your control—markets, timing, other people's recognition, luck.

But if the vocation is just "be good," that simplifies everything. You can do that today. In your current job. In your current circumstances. With whatever resources you have. Being good doesn't require permission, doesn't require recognition, doesn't require perfect conditions. It just requires choosing it.

How to Apply This Today

Before getting caught up in whether your work is impressive enough, visible enough, significant enough—ask a simpler question: "Am I being good in how I'm doing this?" Good meaning honest, fair, careful, kind. If yes, you're fulfilling your vocation regardless of what else happens.

"Perfection of character: to live your last day, every day, without frenzy, or sloth, or pretense."

Perfectio morum: singulis diebus tamquam ultimo vivere, sine tumultu, sine inertia, sine simulatione.

What Marcus Aurelius Meant

Three things that distort character, three things to eliminate: frenzy (the chaos of trying to do everything, impress everyone, secure every possible outcome), sloth (the laziness that comes from thinking you have unlimited time to get serious), and pretense (the performance you put on to manage how others see you).

Live each day as if it's your last, not in the sense of cramming in dramatic experiences, but in the sense of showing up without those three distortions. No frantic scrambling. No lazy postponement. No performing for an audience.

What's left when you remove those? Your actual character. Not the image you're trying to project, not the person you think you should be, but who you actually are when you're not distorting yourself for effect or avoiding the work because you think there's always tomorrow.

Why This Still Matters

Pretense is exhausting. Managing your image, curating how you're perceived, making sure people see you the right way—it takes constant energy and creates constant anxiety. Did they notice? Did it land right? Are they forming the right opinion?

Living without pretense doesn't mean being carelessly authentic or refusing to be professional. It means showing up as yourself, doing your work, letting your character speak through your actions rather than through careful image management. It's simpler, more honest, and creates less friction between who you are and who you're trying to appear to be.

How to Apply This Today

Identify one way you're performing today—one area where you're managing how you appear rather than just being and doing. Drop it. Just for today. Show up without the performance. See if the relief of not pretending outweighs whatever you thought you'd gain from the pretense.

"Everything is only for a day, both that which remembers and that which is remembered."

Omnia ephemera sunt, et quod meminit et quod memoria tenetur.

What Marcus Aurelius Meant

The person doing the remembering? Temporary. The thing being remembered? Temporary. The act of remembering itself? Temporary. The whole system of legacy and memory is built on components that don't last.

You work to be remembered. By whom? By people who will themselves be forgotten. The chain of memory has no permanent anchor. Eventually everyone who remembered you will be gone. Everyone who remembered them will be gone. The whole lineage of remembering dissolves.

Marcus is pulling the foundation out from under the legacy project. Not to make you despair, but to make you stop investing effort in something structurally incapable of delivering what it promises.

Why This Still Matters

The legacy project consumes enormous amounts of energy. Planning how you'll be remembered. Shaping your narrative. Building something that will outlast you. Managing your reputation for people who haven't been born yet.

But those future people won't last either. And neither will their memory of you. And neither will anyone's memory of their memory. At some point, it all dissolves into nothing. Knowing that upfront lets you stop working for an audience that doesn't exist and start working for the reality in front of you.

How to Apply This Today

When you catch yourself making a decision based on how it'll look to posterity, to your legacy, to how you'll be remembered—stop and ask: "What would I do if I knew for certain none of this would be remembered?" Then do that instead.

PART VI

APPLYING STOIC WISDOM TODAY

11

Practicing Stoicism in Daily Life

Understanding Stoicism doesn't make you Stoic any more than understanding nutrition makes you healthy.

You can read every word Marcus Aurelius wrote, grasp every concept perfectly, agree with all of it, and still operate exactly as you did before. Knowledge changes nothing by itself. Practice changes everything.

Stoicism is a set of practices to repeat until they become reflex. Small actions, done consistently, in ordinary moments when nobody's watching and nothing dramatic is at stake. That's where the work actually happens.

Marcus wrote reminders to himself about specific situations: how to handle irritation in the morning, what to remember before a difficult meeting, how to think about setbacks when they arrived. Concrete practices for real moments.

This chapter collects those practices as a working toolkit. Things you can actually do today, in whatever situation you're facing. Each reflection offers a small adjustment in how you meet ordinary circumstances—the kind of adjustment that, repeated enough times, changes how you operate.

The test is whether you use them when it would be easier not to.

"When you wake up in the morning, tell yourself: the people I deal with today will be meddling, ungrateful, arrogant, dishonest, jealous, and surly. They are like this because they can't tell good from evil. But I have recognized that the wrongdoer has a nature related to my own. And so none of them can hurt me."

Cum mane surrexeris, dic tibi: hodie cum hominibus molestis, ingratis, arrogantibus congressurus sum. Ita sunt quia bonum a malo discernere non possunt. Sed ego cognovi naturam malefici meae esse cognatum. Et ideo nemo mihi nocere potest.

What Marcus Aurelius Meant

This is a morning practice, a pre-game preparation for what's coming. Marcus isn't being pessimistic—he's being realistic. You will encounter difficult people today. People who frustrate you, who don't appreciate your effort, who act selfishly or dishonestly. That's not a possibility. It's a certainty.

The practice is reminding yourself of this before it happens, so you're not shocked or destabilized when it does. They're not like this to hurt you personally. They're like this because they can't see clearly—they're confused about what's actually good and what's actually harmful. And because they share your human nature, they deserve patience rather than anger.

The last part is the protection: none of them can actually hurt you unless you let their behavior define your internal state. They can inconvenience you, disappoint you, make things harder. But hurt your character, damage your integrity, force you to act badly? That power doesn't exist unless you grant it.

Why This Still Matters

Most people start their days expecting smooth cooperation and then feel personally attacked when they encounter difficulty or resistance. That gap between expectation and reality creates frustration that compounds throughout the day.

Starting with realistic expectations—yes, you'll encounter selfishness, ingratitude, dishonesty—removes the shock factor. It doesn't make you cynical. It makes you prepared. You can still hope for better, but you're not destabilized when worse appears.

How to Apply This Today

Tomorrow morning, before you check your phone or start your day, spend thirty seconds on this practice. Remind yourself: today will include difficulty from others. That's normal. It doesn't mean anything's wrong. It doesn't require anger. Just recognition and patience.

"The cucumber is bitter? Then throw it out. There are brambles in the path? Then go around. That's all you need to know."

Cucumis amarus est? Proice. Vepres in via sunt? Deverte. Sufficit.

What Marcus Aurelius Meant

Simple problems deserve simple solutions. The cucumber tastes bad—you don't need to hold a meeting about it, analyze why cucumbers have disappointed you, or make it mean something about your life. Just throw it out and move on.

There's an obstacle in your path—you don't need to stand there resenting it, demanding it shouldn't exist, or making its presence into a larger problem. Go around it. Problem solved.

Marcus is pointing to a pattern: we take simple problems and complicate them by adding layers of interpretation, emotion, and significance they don't deserve. The cucumber is just a bad cucumber. The brambles are just obstacles. Deal with them at that level and move on.

Why This Still Matters

People turn minor inconveniences into major emotional events. The coffee's cold, and suddenly it's a story about how nothing goes right. Traffic's bad, and it becomes evidence that the universe is against you. Small problems get upgraded to meaningful grievances.

The practice is keeping small problems small. Notice them, handle them at the appropriate level, move on. Not every difficulty needs deep processing or emotional investment. Most just need a practical response.

How to Apply This Today

Next time a minor problem appears, catch yourself before you escalate it. Is this actually significant, or is this just a bitter cucumber? If it's the latter, handle it simply and let it go. Throw it out. Go around. Move on.

"The first rule is to keep an untroubled spirit. The second is to look things in the face and know them for what they are."

Prima lex: spiritum imperturbatum serva. Secunda: res ut sunt intuere et cognosce.

What Marcus Aurelius Meant

Two practices, in order. First: protect your internal calm. That's the foundation everything else builds on. If you lose that, everything becomes harder—judgment degrades, reactions intensify, small problems feel massive.

Second: see reality clearly. Not how you wish things were, not how they should be, not through the filter of what you want to be true. Just what's actually there, as accurately as you can perceive it.

The order matters. Maintain calm first, then assess clearly. Not the other way around. If you try to see clearly while agitated, your vision is already distorted. The untroubled spirit creates the conditions for accurate perception.

Why This Still Matters

Most people do this backward. They let events disturb them first, then try to figure out what's happening while already upset. That guarantees poor judgment—you're assessing from a compromised state.

The practice is protecting calm first, assessment second. When something potentially disturbing happens, the immediate response isn't analysis or reaction. It's stabilization. Get steady, then look at what's actually there.

How to Apply This Today

Next time something potentially upsetting occurs, pause before you analyze it. First: stabilize. Take three slow breaths. Let the initial spike of emotion settle. Only then: assess. What's actually happening here, without the distortion of the first reaction?

"Objective judgment, now, at this very moment. Unselfish action, now, at this very moment. Willing acceptance, now, at this very moment, of all external events. That's all you need."

Iudicium rectum nunc, in hoc ipso momento. Actio non egoistica nunc, in hoc ipso momento. Acceptatio volens nunc, in hoc ipso momento, omnium externorum. Sufficit.

What Marcus Aurelius Meant

Three practices, all happening in the present moment. Not eventually, not when conditions improve, not after you've prepared more. Now.

Objective judgment: see what's happening without adding your preferences, fears, or interpretations. Just the facts, as clearly as you can perceive them.

Unselfish action: respond based on what the situation needs, not on what protects your ego or serves your immediate interests.

Willing acceptance: receive external events without resistance. Not passive resignation—willing acceptance. You're choosing to work with what's there rather than fighting the fact that it exists.

All three, right now. That's the entire practice. Nothing else is required.

Why This Still Matters

People wait to practice these things until they feel ready, until the stakes are lower, until they've mastered them in easier situations. But the practice is always now. The moment in front of you is the training ground.

You don't get better at objective judgment by planning to be objective later. You get better by practicing it now, in this moment, with whatever's actually happening. Same with unselfish action and willing acceptance. The practice is immediate or it's not practice at all.

How to Apply This Today

In your next challenging moment, run through these three quickly: Am I seeing this objectively? Am I acting from what's needed or what protects me? Am I accepting what's here or fighting its existence? Three questions. Present moment. That's the practice.

"Don't be overheard complaining, not even to yourself."

Ne querelam emittas, ne ad te ipsum.

What Marcus Aurelius Meant

The standard is higher than you think. It's not just about not complaining to other people—that's basic courtesy. It's not complaining even internally, even in your own mind where nobody else can hear.

Why? Because internal complaint has the same effect as external complaint: it reinforces dissatisfaction, rehearses grievance, trains your mind to focus on what's wrong. It doesn't matter if you say it out loud or just think it repeatedly. The pattern gets strengthened either way.

Marcus is asking for discipline not just in speech but in thought. When complaint arises—and it will—notice it and let it go rather than rehearsing it, building on it, turning it into a narrative.

Why This Still Matters

People monitor their external speech but let their internal dialogue run wild. You don't complain to your coworkers, but you spend the commute home rehearsing everything wrong with the day. You don't criticize your family out loud, but mentally you're building a case about how they don't appreciate you.

That internal complaint does damage even if it never becomes external. It shapes your emotional baseline, trains your attention toward grievance, makes dissatisfaction your default state. The practice is catching it internally before it gets that far.

How to Apply This Today

Today, monitor your internal dialogue. When you catch yourself mentally complaining—about traffic, about a person, about how things should be different—notice it and redirect. Not suppression. Just: noticed, redirected. Do that enough times and the habit weakens.

"People exist for the sake of one another. Teach them then or bear with them."

Homines ad se invicem nati sunt. Doce igitur aut tolera.

What Marcus Aurelius Meant

Two options when people frustrate you, annoy you, or act in ways you think are wrong. Either teach them—help them see better, offer guidance, provide the information or perspective they're missing. Or bear with them—accept their limitations, let them be wrong, extend patience without trying to fix them.

What's not an option: resent them. Get angry at them for being who they are. Demand they change to suit your preferences. That's not on the list because it doesn't work and it makes you worse.

Teaching requires that they're willing to learn and that you can actually help. If either condition isn't met, you default to bearing with them. Not bitterly, not while broadcasting your moral superiority. Just: they're like this, that's reality, I can work with reality.

Why This Still Matters

Most interpersonal frustration comes from a third option people keep trying even though it never works: being angry that the person isn't different. You can't change someone through resentment. You can't fix them through irritation. You can only make yourself miserable while they continue exactly as they were.

Teach or tolerate gives you two constructive paths. If you can help them improve, do it. If you can't or they're not interested, accept them as they are and figure out how to work with that reality.

How to Apply This Today

Next time someone frustrates you, immediately ask: "Can I teach them something useful here, or do I need to bear with them?" If teach, do it kindly. If bear, do it without resentment. Those are the only two moves.

"It's time you realized that you have something in you more powerful and miraculous than the things that affect you and make you dance like a puppet."

Tempus est ut intelligas te habere in te aliquid potentius et mirabilius quam ea quae te afficiunt et quasi pupam agitant.

What Marcus Aurelius Meant

External events pull your strings—something happens and you react, someone says something and you respond, circumstances change and you adjust. Like a puppet jerking in response to whatever's pulling the strings at the moment.

But there's something in you that's more powerful than all of that: your capacity for judgment, for deliberate choice, for deciding how to respond rather than just reacting. That faculty can observe what's happening, assess it, and choose a response that comes from your principles rather than from the stimulus.

Marcus is reminding himself that he's not just a puppet dancing to external forces. He has the ability to pause, to think, to choose. That ability is more powerful than whatever's trying to make him react.

Why This Still Matters

Most of daily life operates in reactive mode. Email arrives, you respond. Someone criticizes, you defend. Traffic slows, you get frustrated. The puppet strings get pulled and you dance accordingly, automatically, without engaging the part of you that could choose otherwise.

The practice is remembering you have that choice. You're not forced to react in predictable ways. You can pause, assess, and respond deliberately. That power exists and is accessible, but only if you remember it's there.

How to Apply This Today

Next time you feel yourself reacting automatically—anger rising, defense activating, frustration building—pause and remember: there's something in you more powerful than this trigger. You can observe this reaction without being controlled by it. You can choose a response rather than just executing the automatic one.

12

Living Quietly, Firmly, and Well

Not every good life is visible.

Much of what matters most happens without witnesses: choices made quietly, restraint exercised without recognition, effort applied where no one's keeping score. Marcus Aurelius understood this well. He lived in public, but the work that mattered to him was often done in private.

For Marcus, living well meant being reliable. Steady in judgment. Measured in response. Consistent in effort. A life lived this way **doesn't** require confirmation. It stands on its own.

Quiet can be active. Firm can be humane. And living well requires both—the quietness that protects judgment from noise, the firmness that holds to principle under pressure.

A quiet life **isn't** pulled apart by reaction. A firm life is guided by principle rather than impulse. Together, they describe a way of living that holds even when conditions are imperfect and attention is absent.

This chapter stays with what has already been shown: acting with care, accepting limits, judging clearly, and letting results fall where they may. Nothing more is required.

That, for Marcus Aurelius, was enough.

"Get straight to the task at hand. Stop letting your eyes wander. Stop listening to gossip. Stop concerning yourself with other people's business."

Ad opus quod ante te est recta perge. Oculos vagari desine. Rumoribus aures praebere desine. Aliena curare desine.

What Marcus Aurelius Meant

Four commands, all variations on the same instruction: stop looking elsewhere. Your eyes want to check who's watching. Your ears want to track what's being said. Your mind wants to monitor what others are doing. All of that pulls attention away from the work directly in front of you.

Marcus isn't describing isolation. He's describing focus protected from distraction. The task at hand deserves your full attention, but it rarely gets it because attention keeps drifting outward—checking for reactions, measuring against others, consuming information that has nothing to do with what you're actually responsible for.

Getting straight to the task means cutting through all of that and directing energy where it can actually accomplish something. Not because external things don't exist, but because they don't belong to what you're doing right now.

Why This Still Matters

The modern environment makes wandering attention feel productive. You're "staying informed," "keeping up," "being aware of what's happening." But most of that information doesn't improve your actual work—it just creates the feeling of being busy while actual progress stalls.

Attention is finite. Every moment spent tracking gossip, monitoring others, or checking how your work is being received is a moment not spent on the work itself. The task suffers not because you don't care, but because you're dividing limited resources across too many targets.

How to Apply This Today

For the next task you do, eliminate one category of distraction completely. Don't check notifications. Don't look at who else is working on what. Don't monitor reactions. Just the task. See if the quality changes when attention stops splitting.

"Soon you'll be dead, and your life still incomplete. You still treat yourself as second priority."

Brevi morieris, et nondum vita tua perfecta est. Adhuc te ipsum in secundo loco ponis.

What Marcus Aurelius Meant

You're running out of time and you're still not prioritizing yourself. Not in the selfish sense—prioritizing your own development, your own character, your own integrity. You keep putting that work second to everything else: other people's needs, external demands, the urgency of the moment, whatever feels pressing right now.

Death is coming whether you're ready or not, whether your life feels complete or not. And if you keep treating your own character development as something to get to later, after everything else is handled, you'll run out of time before you ever get to it. The urgent will continue consuming all available attention, and the important work—becoming who you're capable of being—will remain perpetually postponed.

Marcus isn't being morbid. He's being precise. You have limited time. Using it to maintain everyone else's approval while neglecting your own development is a choice, and it's the wrong choice.

Why This Still Matters

People structure their lives around external demands and treat their own development as optional. Work needs doing, people need helping, responsibilities need meeting—all of that comes first. Self-improvement, character work, becoming better—that waits for free time that never arrives.

The result is lives spent being useful to others while never actually growing into the person you could be. You're reliable, you're helpful, you're responsive—and you're stuck in exactly the same patterns, the same weaknesses, the same limitations you had ten years ago because you never made yourself the priority.

How to Apply This Today

Block one hour this week—actually put it in your calendar—for your own development. Not productivity. Not helping others. Just: what would make you better? Reading that matters. Reflection. Practice of a skill that's atrophied. Treat that hour as non-negotiable as any external obligation.

"If you've done your best, what else is there?"

Si quantum poteras fecisti, quid amplius?

What Marcus Aurelius Meant

There's a point where effort legitimately ends. Most people don't reach it because they're waiting for external confirmation that they've done enough—approval, success, recognition that the work mattered. Marcus is placing that endpoint earlier, inside your own judgment.

If you acted with care, with honesty, with your full attention and capability, then you're done. The work is complete. What happens after—whether it succeeds, whether anyone notices, whether it produces the results you hoped for—that's separate from whether you did your part well.

This isn't permission to be sloppy or quit early. It's recognition that obsessing over outcomes you can't control doesn't improve anything. It just keeps you tethered to work that's already finished, preventing closure and consuming energy that could go toward what's next.

Why This Still Matters

Perfectionism disguises itself as high standards, but often it's just an inability to let work end. There's always something more to check, adjust, improve, explain. That creates projects that never finish, conversations that never close, decisions that keep getting revisited.

Learning to ask "Did I do my best with what I had?" and accepting "yes" as an answer creates the ability to complete things. Not perfectly—completely. There's a difference, and the second one is actually achievable.

How to Apply This Today

After your next piece of significant work, ask honestly: "Did I give this my full capability?" If yes, let it be done. Don't revisit it for reassurance. Don't wait for validation. Just move to what's next.

"Stop whatever you're doing for a moment and ask yourself: Am I afraid of death because I won't be able to do this anymore?"

Desiste paulisper ab opere et te interroga: Mortemne timeo quia hoc amplius facere non potero?

What Marcus Aurelius Meant

Test what you're doing against mortality. If you couldn't do this anymore—if death arrived tomorrow—would that be the tragedy? Would the inability to continue this specific activity be what you'd regret?

Usually the answer is no. The activity itself isn't what matters—it's whether you're doing it well, whether it aligns with who you've decided to be, whether it contributes something meaningful. If you're doing work you'd be embarrassed to have as your final act, that's information worth having now, while you can still change course.

This isn't about making every moment profound. It's about using mortality as a filter for what deserves your limited time and what's just filling space.

Why This Still Matters

People spend enormous amounts of time on things they wouldn't choose if they were honest about their finitude. Work that feels obligatory but serves no real purpose. Relationships maintained out of habit rather than care. Tasks that consume hours without moving anything forward.

The question "Would I regret not being able to do this?" cuts through rationalization quickly. If the answer is no, you're either doing it badly or doing the wrong thing. Either way, that's useful information.

How to Apply This Today

Look at how you spent today. Pick the activity that consumed the most time. Ask: "If I died tomorrow, would my inability to continue this be the loss?" If no, that activity needs either better execution or elimination.

"No matter what anyone says or does, my task is to be good. Like gold or emerald or purple would say: whatever anyone says or does, my task is to be emerald and keep my color true."

Quidquid alii dicant aut faciant, mihi bonum esse opus est. Sicut aurum vel smaragdus vel purpura diceret: quidquid alii dicant aut faciant, mihi smaragdum esse et colorem meum servare opus est.

What Marcus Aurelius Meant

Emerald doesn't stop being emerald because someone criticizes it or because another gem seems more impressive. Its task—its nature—is to maintain its particular quality regardless of external response. You have the same task: to be good, to maintain your character, independent of how that's received.

Other people will have opinions. Circumstances will create pressure. Easier options will appear attractive. None of that changes your fundamental task, which is acting with integrity according to the principles you've chosen. Like the emerald keeping its color, you keep your character—not because anyone's watching, not because it'll be rewarded, but because that's what you're here to do.

Why This Still Matters

Character bends under pressure from environment, from peer behavior, from what seems acceptable in a given context. You act one way when you're alone, another when you're being watched, a third when the stakes are high. That inconsistency creates internal friction.

Having a task that doesn't change regardless of conditions—"my task is to be good"—creates stability. It's the same in every situation, which means you don't have to recalculate constantly based on who's present or what's at stake.

How to Apply This Today

Before your next decision, especially one where pressure or opportunity is creating temptation to compromise, remind yourself: "My task is to be good. Just that. Nothing else is required." Then choose accordingly.

"Someone despises me. That's their problem. Mine is not to do or say anything despicable."

Aliquis me contemnit. Eius res est. Mea est ne quid contemptibile faciam aut dicam.

What Marcus Aurelius Meant

When someone judges you negatively, two separate things are happening. Their judgment—that's their business, their responsibility, their problem to manage. Your conduct—that's your business, your responsibility, your only actual concern.

Marcus is drawing a hard boundary. You can't control their opinion. You can't make them think well of you. You can't force respect or appreciation. All of that lives on their side of the line. What lives on your side is simpler: don't act or speak in ways that are actually despicable.

If you've maintained that standard, their contempt says something about them, not about you. If you haven't maintained it, their opinion is irrelevant—you already know you acted poorly.

Why This Still Matters

People waste enormous energy trying to change others' negative opinions through explanation, defense, or proving their worth. None of that works reliably, and all of it creates dependence on external validation.

The alternative is simpler: act with integrity, then let others think what they think. If their judgment is wrong, that's their error to carry. If it's right, you already know it and can address it directly rather than through managing their perception.

How to Apply This Today

Next time you catch yourself trying to change someone's negative opinion of you, stop and ask: "Did I act despicably?" If no, let their opinion be their problem. If yes, address the behavior, not the perception.

"Be content with your lot, and rejoice in the way things are. When you realize there is nothing lacking, the whole world belongs to you."

Sorte tua contentus esto, et in rebus ut sunt gaude. Cum intelligis nihil deesse, totus mundus tuus est.

What Marcus Aurelius Meant

Wanting things to be different from how they are creates constant tension. You're always measuring reality against preference, always finding it insufficient, always waiting for conditions to improve before you can feel satisfied. Marcus is describing the alternative: accepting what is, finding contentment there, recognizing that "lacking" is usually a story rather than a fact.

This isn't resignation or settling. It's the recognition that your current circumstances, however imperfect, contain everything necessary for you to act well right now. You don't need different resources, better conditions, or changed situations to live with integrity. What you have is enough for what actually matters.

Why This Still Matters

The gap between "what is" and "what should be" consumes endless mental energy. Things should be easier. People should be different. Circumstances should have worked out better. That constant comparison creates dissatisfaction that colors everything, even moments that would otherwise be fine.

Closing that gap—not by changing external reality but by accepting it as workable—creates immediate relief. You're no longer waiting for life to cooperate before you can operate well. You're working with what's here, which is all you ever actually have.

How to Apply This Today

Identify one thing about your current situation you keep wishing were different. Ask honestly: "Can I act well despite this, or does this actually prevent good action?" Usually it doesn't prevent anything. It just makes things less comfortable. That discomfort is manageable. Let it be.

"Keep yourself simple, good, pure, serious, unassuming, a friend of justice, god-fearing, kind, affectionate, strong for your proper work. Strive your hardest to remain the same person philosophy wished to make you."

Simplex esto, bonus, sincerus, gravis, non superbus, iustitiae amicus, pius, benignus, amans, ad opus tuum aptum fortis. Maxime contende ut maneás qualis te philosophia esse voluit.

What Marcus Aurelius Meant

This is the fullest description Marcus offers of what he's working toward. Not one quality but many, held together, practiced consistently. Simple—free from unnecessary complexity. Good—acting with integrity. Pure—honest in motivation. Serious—treating what matters with appropriate weight. Unassuming—without pretense or inflation.

A friend of justice, kind, affectionate, strong for the actual work in front of you. And then the crucial part: strive to remain the person philosophy wished to make you. Not to become someone new constantly, but to maintain the character you've already developed through practice.

Why This Still Matters

People treat character as something that needs constant reinvention. New self-improvement projects. Different approaches. Changed identities. But character work is more about consistency than novelty. It's about becoming someone and then being that person reliably, across changing circumstances, without constant drift or backsliding.

The list Marcus provides isn't aspirational—it's descriptive of what he's already practiced. The challenge is staying there, not achieving it once. That's harder than it sounds, because pressure constantly pushes toward compromise, toward expedience, toward easier versions of yourself.

How to Apply This Today

Write down three qualities you've already developed through practice—ways you've learned to show up that represent your best character. Your only job today is maintaining those three. Not improving them, not adding more. Just: be who you've already learned to be.

Appendix - Historical and Cultural Context

Marcus Aurelius was born in Rome in 121 CE and ruled as Roman emperor from 161 until his death in 180. He didn't seek the position. It arrived through adoption and succession, carrying obligations he couldn't refuse and pressures he couldn't escape.

His day-to-day reality combined political leadership, military command, judicial decisions, and constant public visibility. People watched how he walked, what he said, whether he showed impatience or fatigue. Composure wasn't optional—it was part of the job. A bad mood in the emperor could destabilize entire provinces.

Authority was extensive but never absolute. He commanded legions, but logistics moved at the speed of horses and ships. He issued decrees, but local governors interpreted them differently. He made decisions with incomplete information, knowing that by the time messengers returned with updates, circumstances had already changed.

The *Meditations* come from this context: someone at the center of power, trying to maintain clarity under conditions that actively worked against it. These aren't the reflections of a philosopher who withdrew from the world to think. They're the working notes of someone who had to keep functioning while the world pressed in from every direction.

The Roman World of the Second Century

By Marcus's time, the Roman Empire stretched from Britain to Egypt, from Spain to Syria. Three continents. Dozens of languages. Hundreds of cities, each with its own local politics, rivalries, and expectations of what Rome owed them.

Holding this together required constant attention to problems that multiplied faster than they could be solved. A grain shortage in Alexandria meant potential riots. A dispute between two cities in Asia Minor could escalate into violence if not mediated quickly. Barbarian movements along the Rhine and Danube required military response before they became invasions.

Communication moved slowly. A message from the eastern frontier took weeks to reach Rome. By the time Marcus received information and sent back instructions, the situation had often evolved into something different. He was governing in the past, making decisions about problems that had already shifted.

Public expectation added another layer. Citizens saw the emperor as personally responsible for everything—military victories, food prices, whether the gods were pleased. When things went wrong, they blamed him. When things went right, they expected more. The job had no clear boundaries and no moment where you could say the work was done.

Crisis as Normal Operating Conditions

Marcus ruled during nineteen years of nearly continuous crisis.

The northern frontiers—modern-day Germany, Austria, Hungary—required constant military presence. Germanic tribes and Sarmatian cavalry weren't launching one invasion that could be defeated and forgotten. They were testing the borders repeatedly, probing for weakness, raiding when opportunity appeared. Marcus spent over a decade on campaign, living in military camps, dealing with supply problems, disease outbreaks among his troops, and the grinding reality that victories rarely lasted.

Then the plague arrived. The Antonine Plague, likely smallpox, entered the empire around 165 CE and kept returning. It killed millions—maybe a quarter of the population in some regions. The army lost soldiers faster than they could be replaced.

Economic production collapsed in affected areas. Tax revenue dried up exactly when the military needed more funding.

Marcus had to govern through this. Make decisions about troop deployments when half the legion was sick. Manage the economy when labor had disappeared. Maintain public confidence when people were dying in numbers that made it obvious the emperor couldn't protect them.

Political succession added another weight. His son Commodus was his heir—a son Marcus knew wasn't fit for the role but couldn't bypass without risking civil war. Every decision about Commodus's education, his public role, his exposure to power carried the knowledge that this person would eventually inherit an empire he wasn't capable of managing.

This wasn't crisis as interruption. This was crisis as the permanent condition of work.

Education and Cultural Formation

Marcus received the best education money and status could buy in the Roman world. Multiple tutors in rhetoric, literature, law, Greek philosophy. Training in public speaking, since emperors were expected to address the Senate, the army, and public assemblies with clarity and authority.

But this wasn't education for its own sake. It was formation for public life. You learned philosophy not to become a philosopher but to develop self-control, clear judgment, and the ability to maintain composure under pressure. You studied rhetoric so you could persuade, command, and project authority when needed.

Greek culture dominated the intellectual life of Rome's elite. Educated Romans read Greek literature, wrote philosophy in Greek, and used Greek as the language of serious reflection. Latin was for law, administration, and military command. Greek was for thinking.

This split mattered for the *Meditations*. When Marcus wanted to think carefully about how to act, he wrote in Greek. It created distance from his role as emperor, which operated in Latin. The language itself helped separate public performance from private reflection.

Writing Practices in the Ancient World

Personal notebooks were common among educated Romans. These weren't diaries in the modern sense—they were working tools. Places to record useful quotes, test out arguments, remind yourself of principles you kept forgetting, work through problems that had no clear solution.

The point was use, not preservation. Nobody expected these notes to be read by others. They were rough, repetitive, unpolished—whatever helped you think more clearly or maintain discipline when it threatened to slip.

This tradition explains the *Meditations'* form. Why the same ideas appear multiple times. Why some entries are polished and others feel unfinished. Why there's no clear organization or narrative arc. These were notes Marcus wrote for himself, to himself, when he needed to steady his judgment or remind himself how to act under pressure.

The title *Meditations* was added centuries later. Marcus called his notes *Ta eis heauton*—"things to himself." That's what they were: reminders, corrections, attempts to think clearly when circumstances were making that difficult.

The Language of the *Meditations*

Marcus wrote in Greek, not Latin. For a Roman emperor, this choice signals something important: these notes weren't official, weren't public, weren't part of governance.

Greek was the language educated Romans used for philosophy and self-examination. It carried associations with reflection, restraint, and careful thinking that Latin—the language of law and military commands—didn't have in quite the same way.

Writing in Greek also created useful distance. When Marcus wrote in Latin, he was the emperor issuing decrees, commanding armies, rendering judgments. When he wrote in Greek, he could step back from that role and examine his own thinking without the weight of imperial authority pressing on every sentence.

The result is a voice that's measured, deliberate, and intensely focused inward. Not the voice of someone addressing subjects or soldiers, but someone working through problems alone, trying to figure out how to keep functioning well under impossible conditions.

Where and When the Notes Were Written

The *Meditations* weren't written in a study during peaceful moments of reflection. Most were likely composed during military campaigns along the Danube frontier—modern-day Austria, Hungary, Slovakia—where Marcus spent years commanding armies, managing supply lines, dealing with tribal negotiations and battle casualties.

He wrote in military camps, in temporary quarters, between meetings with generals and messengers bringing news from other fronts. Sometimes while sick—Marcus dealt with chronic health problems that military life made worse. Sometimes while exhausted from travel, from decisions that had to be made without enough information, from the grinding awareness that the war would probably outlast him.

The conditions show in the writing. Brief entries that feel like they were grabbed during a short break. Repetitive ideas that suggest he kept returning to the same problems because they kept reappearing. Fragmentary thoughts that start strong and then trail off, as if he was interrupted mid-sentence.

There was no dedicated time for reflection, no quiet room where philosophy happened separate from command. Marcus had to think clearly while everything around him demanded immediate response. The *Meditations* reflect that tension—the attempt to maintain composure and judgment while operating in an environment designed to destroy both.

Preservation, Transmission, and Historical Distance

Marcus never prepared these notes for publication. He didn't organize them, edit them, or arrange them into a coherent structure. They were his private working notes, and he had no reason to think anyone else would read them.

How they survived is unclear. Someone—a family member, an aide, possibly someone who found them after his death—recognized their value and preserved them. The notes were copied by hand, passed along, copied again. Each time someone copied the manuscript, they made small decisions: which entries to include, how to group them, where to start and stop sections.

Over centuries, as the text moved through different languages and cultures, it accumulated changes. Translators made choices about tone, emphasis, and vocabulary. Some aimed for literal accuracy. Others prioritized readability. Each version reflects not just Marcus's thinking but also the priorities and assumptions of the people who transmitted it.

The title *Meditations* appeared somewhere in this process—probably in the Renaissance, centuries after Marcus died. The division into twelve "books" might be original, or might have been imposed by medieval copyists looking for organizational structure. We don't know for certain.

What survived is rougher, more uneven, and more fragmented than a text prepared for readers would be. But that roughness is also what makes it valuable. You're reading someone's actual working thoughts, not a polished performance. The repetition, the abruptness, the sudden shifts—those are features of how the notes were actually used, not flaws to be smoothed away.

Understanding this history helps explain why the *Meditations* don't read like a normal book. They weren't meant to. They were meant to work, to help Marcus think clearly under pressure. That they still work for readers two thousand years later, under completely different circumstances, is remarkable. But it helps to know what you're reading: not a philosophy treatise, but a survival manual written by someone trying to remain sane while running an empire during its long decline.

Thanks

Thank you for spending time with this book. Reading is a quiet commitment, and I don't take it lightly. I hope these pages offered something useful—clarity when you needed it, direction when things felt unclear.

My thanks to the team at Karma Studio, whose careful work and steady support helped bring this project to completion. I'm also grateful to Giulio Vitali, author of *Vox Populi*, for his thoughtful guidance and valuable advice throughout the development of this book.

I want to thank my family as well, for their patience and encouragement throughout the writing process. Their support made the long, quiet hours of work possible.

If you found this book helpful, leaving an honest review on Amazon would be deeply appreciated. Reviews help independent authors reach readers who might benefit from work like this.

Thank you again for reading.

— *Richard Lawson*

www.ingramcontent.com/pod-product-compliance
Lightning Source LLC
Chambersburg PA
CBHW061534050726
47593CB00002B/786